Discovering the P

14 Circular Walks of

by
Brian Herd

These routes take the walker through some of the most
breathtaking scenery of the Peak District.

*'All of you with children, take them somehow into the country, among green grass and yellow wheat,
among trees by hills and streams, if you wish their highest education, that of the heart and soul
completed.'*

Richard Jefferies.
1849 - 1887

*who would live turmoiled in the town
when you can enjoy such pleasant walks as these?'*

William Shakespeare.

Map of the Peak District

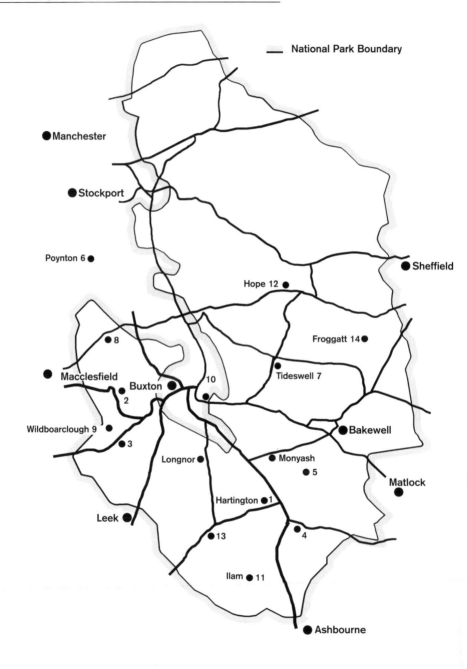

National Park Boundary

Manchester

Stockport

Poynton 6

Sheffield

Hope 12

8

Froggatt 14

Macclesfield

Buxton

2

10

Tideswell 7

Wildboarclough 9

3

Bakewell

Longnor

Monyash

5

Matlock

Hartington 1

Leek

13

4

Ilam 11

Ashbourne

CONTENTS

INTRODUCTION

THE PEAK NATIONAL PARK

The area we know as the Peak District is far more than a scenic, weekend playground for us 'townies'. It is a living, working community and has been for hundreds of years. In the countryside where there are not the same commercial pressures that exist in towns and cities, little changes and particularly in the Peak Park, where regulations exist to restrict unsuitable development. As a consequence much of what we see today is as it was many years ago and the character of the area is relatively unspoilt. Man has lived here since very early times, there are bronze and iron age remains, and evidence still of the Roman occupation. Also much of the beautiful countryside belies an intensive industrial past and once again, there are many places of interest to see. It is all there if we only care to look, but all too often there is nothing to guide the casual visitor to the places of interest or to inform them of some of the more esoteric facts about the area. Perhaps it is considered that the erection of explanatory signboards everywhere would be contrary to the aims of the Peak Park Planning Board and would have a detrimental effect on the natural environment. Whatever the reasons, there is still much to excite the imagination in the area and I hope that this book will go some way towards remedying the situation.

THE WALKS

Whilst some of the locations included in the book are capable of being visited via the road network, many are only accessible on foot and consequently I have compiled a series of walks incorporating as much information as possible about the area where they take place. The experienced Peak District walker will probably already know most of the walks well but what I hope will be new to most readers, is the snippets of information about places or features encountered along the way. Much of the information is historical, covering relics from prehistoric times to the present day. There are tales of ghosts and incredible stories about the folk who lived and worked in the area in the past, their beliefs and customs. There is also information relating to the industrial past, little of which now remains or is recognisable. It is not my intention to educate the reader but merely to make him/her aware that there is much more to the Peak District than just the beautiful scenery and if, after having read the book, your appetite is whetted to discover more, then I shall be more than happy. I hope that you will find my efforts both entertaining and informative and having read the book, that it contributes towards your understanding and enjoyment of the area in the future.

At the beginning of each walk I have included some useful information relating to it. Maps, references, directions and distance can obviously be assumed to be reasonably accurate but of course my assessment of the duration of a walk is intended for guidance only. So, when planning a walk please do not rely entirely upon my estimations. Similarly, my suggestions on refreshment arrangements are not recommendations but merely the places where I chose to stop when I did the walk. You are welcome to follow in my footsteps as it were, but one should of course make arrangements to suit oneself.

SAFETY FIRST

The walks are generally of easy to moderate standard. There are one or two stiff climbs but nothing that should trouble anyone who is reasonably fit. One should be aware however that the weather on the hills, particularly in the Dark Peak area, can change dramatically, rapidly transforming bright and clear to zero visibility or turning the conditions underfoot into a quagmire. If you are not adequately prepared a pleasant stroll can quickly turn into a real hard slog or worse still, a pleasant day's outing can become a nightmare.

When walking in the hills it is always important to remember that the weather can be extreme and it is best to be prepared for the worst rather than suffer the consequences. For this reason, there are certain basic items of equipment that should be regarded as essential and without which one should never venture onto the hills. Be sure to wear good strong shoes or boots with a deep pattern on the sole. Boots are preferable because they give support and protection to the ankles when the terrain is rough as it frequently is.

Protective clothing is equally important. Good quality cagoules and over trousers are recommended to insulate against the wind and rain. One should also carry extra clothing for use in emergencies. Mishaps can happen to the best of us therefore a first-aid kit together with spare food and a hot drink is also advisable.

I have provided a rough sketch map for each of the walks and endeavoured to make the directions as clear and concise as possible but nevertheless I would strongly recommend that a map and compass be used as a backup.

It cannot be stressed enough, that the hills can be dangerous and must be treated with respect. Some knowledge of the mountain code would not go amiss, accidents can happen in the most benign of surroundings and a home contact who can alert the emergency services and inform them of your possible location is essential in the event that you do not return within your planned timescale.

THE ENVIRONMENT

Finally, it should always be remembered that although the countryside is a place of recreation for many of us, there are a great many people who live and work there, and often their very livelihoods could be threatened by the thoughtless actions of individuals ignorant in the ways of country folk. It is obvious therefore, that we should do everything within our power to respect their way of life and do as little as possible to disturb their sometimes fragile existence.

Equally, if we are to preserve our open spaces for our children, then we must also treat the countryside with respect. The Country Code is a guide to good behaviour in the countryside and was compiled to help us protect our heritage. I have reproduced it here in the hope that you will enjoy yourselves whilst at the same time maintaining an amicable relationship with those who are fortunate enough to live there. There is an old adage that we would all do well to remember:

'Take only photographs,
Leave nothing but footprints,
Kill nothing but time.'

THE COUNTRY CODE

Guard against all risk of fire.

Fasten all gates.

Keep dogs under proper control.

Keep to paths across farmland.

Avoid damage to fences,
hedges and walls.

Leave no litter.

Safeguard water supplies.

Protect wildlife, wild plants and trees.

Go carefully on country roads.

Respect the life of the countryside.

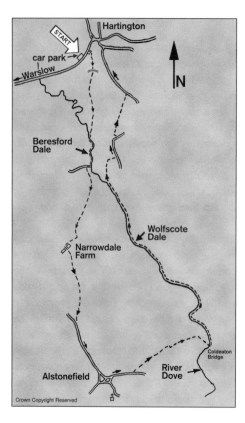

WALK 1

BERESFORD DALE, ALSTONEFIELD AND WOLFSCOTE DALE

Beresford Dale and Wolfscote Dale are the northern reaches of the famous River Dove. Although narrower and not quite as spectacular as Dovedale these dales offer equally splendid walking and being less well known, the peace and solitude here makes this a most attractive route. It is often possible to walk the whole length of the dales without encountering another person. The walk starts from the village of Hartington which though quite large, retains a quaint atmosphere. In contrast, Alstonefield is a quiet picturesque village with grey cottages mostly of eighteenth century origin, but with some earlier examples, grouped around a village green complete with coaching inn. Before moving on to Wolfscote Dale, St. Peter's Church has a number of interesting features and is well worth a visit.

Map:
Ordnance Survey Outdoor Leisure Map 24.

Start:
Car park on the outskirts of Hartington on the Warslow road. Map ref. SK 127 602.

Directions:
Hartington is situated to the West of the A515 Buxton/Ashbourne road and is well signposted.

Distance:
The walk is approximately eight miles (13km).

Duration:
Five to five-and-a-half hours including stops for refreshments and time to explore Alstonefield village.

Refreshments:
A choice of either the Tea Rooms at Alstonefield or *The George Inn* at Alstonefield.

Setting Out

Upon leaving the car park, turn left towards the village and cross the road to the public toilets. The footpath is to be found at the top of a short flight of steps on the left side of the building by a sign indicating 'Dovedale via Beresford Dale and Wolfscote Dale'. The path passes through a gate and bears right over fields before crossing an old walled track. Continue over the fields on a well-defined path until you eventually reach a small gate which gives access to a wood. Here the path joins the banks of the River Dove in Beresford Dale.

Beresford Dale

Much of the White Peak and the River Dove in particular, was the haunt of that most famous of anglers, Izaak Walton, and his book '*The Compleat Angler*', which was published in 1676, relates many of his experiences in the area. He often stayed at nearby Beresford Hall, sadly long since demolished, as a guest of his close friend and fishing partner Charles Cotton. As you enter the wood look to your right and you will see across the river, amidst the trees, their 'fishing temple' which still remains.

Follow the path through the wood until a footbridge is reached, just beyond which is Pike Pool named after the tall thin pinnacle of rock in the river, not the fish as might have been expected. Cross the bridge and continue along the opposite bank. The dale here is narrow and leafy and the river abounds with ducks and wildfowl, it is certainly one of the most beautiful spots in the Peak District.

Upon reaching another footbridge at the end of the dale do not cross but instead, turn right and enter a lane only to leave it again almost immediately through a gate on the left, opposite Beresford House. The path proceeds up the field with a wall and hedge on the right and soon becomes a wide track. It ascends gradually round the right of the hill towards Narrowdale and after passing through a number of gates the track is joined by another on the right.

Narrowdale Farm

Take this track and walk up to Narrowdale Farm, once a quite picturesque place but now sadly neglected. Turn left between the buildings and go through a gate. Follow the wall on the left up the field until the path is joined by another through a stile in the wall, at this point bear right, away from the wall and walk up the field to the lip of the dale. The path here affords fine views over the dale and looking back, Hartington and the hills of Sheen can be seen in the distance.

The path now moves away from the dale alongside a wall on the right and crosses a series of fields towards a small copse. Pass through two stiles and cross an old walled track before passing a copse on your right. The path crosses another stile and continues in a straight line to emerge at a road at yet another stile. Turn left and walk down the road towards the village. As you approach, notice the old water pump beside the road on the right.

Alstonefield

A settlement has stood here since very early times, the first documented evidence being in the year 892. The origin of the name Alstonefield has given rise to a great deal of speculation but in the Domesday Book it is referred to as Aenestanefelt, meaning 'Aelfstan's Felled' (land free from woodland). At the junction at the bottom of the road, turn to the left and then immediately right at the village green, the centre of the village.

Alstonefield is an attractive village if a little isolated, it only acquired piped water in the nineteen-fifties. Most of the buildings date from the eighteenth century but the Hall is by far the oldest having been built in 1574. At one time a wool market used to be held behind the inn and a silk mill is reputed to have been active here. One of the larger buildings, now converted into a private home, was a workhouse in the nineteenth century. It housed about fifty paupers and it also had a ward which served as an early lunatic asylum.

Lunch can be obtained at *The George*, once a coaching inn, or at the nearby coffee shops or tea rooms, however before leaving the village a visit to St. Peter's Church is recommended.

St. Peter's Church

From the village green, take the Milldale road, passing the old hall on the left. The church is just beyond as the road bears left. This charming old church, like many others in the area, features a variety of architectural styles and much evidence exists to indicate that the site has been a place of worship for a great many years. The earliest report of a church being here was in the year 892 when a dedication ceremony was held by St. Oswald, the then Archbishop of York. At the time he was touring the North of England together with other Bishops with the intention of reinforcing the Faith following a resurgence of paganism.

There are a number of fragments of Saxon crosses evident here principally in the right hand side wall of the porch where they were obviously used during a period of rebuilding. Also, to the left of the porch, and still standing in the churchyard, is the base of yet another Saxon cross. They probably date from the early part of the tenth century and there are so many fragments with different patterns that it has been speculated that a workshop may have been sited here, supplying crosses to the surrounding area.

Before entering, take a walk around the outside of the church. Notice the date and the initials LB carved either side of the window at the back of the building. This is to commemorate the rebuilding of the chancel in 1590 by Laurence Beresford. The South porch, built about 1300, has an unusual roof fashioned from stone rather than the slate which is normally used. The inner doorway is typically Norman with its rounded arch shape although look again later from the inside when you will see that it is pointed, obviously having been rebuilt at some time. This was at one time the main entrance to the church when the road to Milldale passed on the South rather than the North as it now does.

Finally, look for two small but rather interesting gravestones near to the wall of the churchyard opposite this porch. One is square in shape and is in memory of Margaret Barclay who died in 1731 aged 107. Gravestones indicating that folk had lived to great ages are not particularly uncommon, they can however, rarely be relied upon. The next one though, is very interesting. It is similar to the other one but this has a rounded top. It commemorates the death of Anne Green in April 1518 and, if the date is to be believed, this is perhaps the oldest memorial you are ever likely to see.

Inside the church there are more Saxon remains including the bowl of a font, possibly the forerunner of the modern copy which is currently in use. The most striking thing about the church interior is the marvellous quality of the wood carving. The central banks of pews are particularly ornate and in some cases bear the names of the craftsmen responsible. The majority of the woodwork dates from the early sixteenth century and of particular interest is the somewhat incongruously painted Cotton family pew.

You cannot fail to see this box pew with its unusual blue/green colour and the Cotton coat-of-arms emblazoned on the back. It has obviously been moved from its original position but it can be seen to advantage at the end of the North aisle. It was commissioned by Charles Cotton senior, the then owner of Beresford Hall and father of the Charles Cotton referred to earlier.

After leaving the church, return towards the village green and bear right on the road to Lode Mill. The route now is by way of a footpath on the left. Ignore the first footpath sign and then at the second proceed along a walled track which runs in more or less a straight line between fields and gradually becomes a narrow path which suddenly dog-legs first right and then left to continue to a stile. Climb the stile and bear slightly right to the edge of Wolfscote Dale.

Wolfscote Dale

The path now drops down steeply to the River Dove at Coldeaton Bridge. Although there is little evidence now, the small valley opposite was once the site of a settlement which thrived here until the middle ages. Excavation of a nearby burial mound revealed evidence of an Anglo-Saxon cremation from the period prior to Christianisation. Amongst the remains found were two bone combs, various iron fragments and a number of pieces of bone, believed to have been counters or playing-pieces for some kind of game.

After carefully descending the side of the dale, cross the bridge and follow the river to the left. The name, Wolfscote, is said to derive from 'Wulfstan's cottage' which might indicate that the dale was occupied by Danes at some time. The route through Wolfscote Dale is undoubtedly amongst the most attractive and enjoyable in the Peak. The gentle path beside the Dove, and the steep grassy sides of the dale, sometimes wooded and with occasional towering limestone crags make this a magnificent walk. Coupled with the fact that the dale is still relatively unknown and quiet in comparison to the more popular Dovedale to the south, you have a truly memorable walk.

In a little while a stile is reached at the junction with Biggin Dale, a shallow, dry valley which climbs gradually away to the right. Cross the stile and carry straight on to the left. After walking through the dale for approximately two miles it opens out and a number of caves come into view in the face of the limestone cliffs on the right. It is said that Charles Cotton junior, an inveterate gambler and frequently in debt, used to escape to the dale and spend many an hour hiding in these caves whenever his creditors came calling at the ancestral home, Beresford Hall which he was eventually forced to sell.

Just beyond the caves, cross a stile and turn right up an old walled farm track which rises steadily away from the dale. At the junction, which is encountered almost immediately, continue climbing until the track bends sharply to the right between fields before eventually emerging at a lane. Turn left here and shortly a small round pond will come into view in the field on the left.

These ponds are known as a 'meres' and many of them can be seen in the southern Peak District. In this area where the underlying rock is predominantly limestone, rainwater soon drains away leaving grazing animals with little or nothing to drink. The building of these meres has long provided the solution to the problem and though they are now constructed using a concrete base, in bygone times men used to specialise in creating watertight bases from clay. The problem of water shortage was of such proportions that they were in great demand and travelled far and wide plying their trade.

Follow the lane until just around the bend, a footpath sign to Hartington is seen on the left. This is another walled track and soon after turning sharply to the right it runs in more or less a straight line to a junction at another lane. Turn left again and walk along the lane, heading towards Hartington Church, the tower of which soon comes into view.

Hartington Hall

Upon reaching a T-junction it is worth making a small detour to the right to see Hartington Hall. Built originally in 1350 for the nuns of St. Clare, it was rebuilt in 1611 by Robert Bateman, a local man who became a successful merchant in London. Built as his country residence, it is considered to be one of the finest surviving examples of early Jacobean architecture. It is said that Bonnie Prince Charlie was given shelter here when he

marched his Highlanders through Ashbourne in 1742. It became a Youth Hostel in 1932 and is now one of the Association's most popular hostels.

Hartington

Return down the road and continue on into the village. Hartington was probably an established Anglo Saxon settlement from as early as the 7th or 8th century. First recorded in the Domesday Survey of 1086 as Hortendun meaning 'Heorots Hill', it was one of many estates given to Henry de Ferrers by William the Conqueror. The Duke of Derby once had a castle here but it was confiscated by the Duke of Lancaster in 1265 after the battle of Evesham and has now disappeared completely.

In 1651 a huge battle is believed to have taken place here when 600 Royalist soldiers were ambushed by the predominantly Cromwellian locals as they marched north en route to Wigan. The Royalists were defeated and their commander was fatally wounded. He was supposedly carried off to safety by supporters of the Crown but he eventually died from his injuries and was buried in a wood near the village of Cressbrook some ten-and-a-half miles away. The story goes that in the middle of the last century a farmer erecting a gate post there unearthed a skeleton, still dressed in a well-preserved Royalist uniform and complete with weapons. Upon reaching the main road a visit to St. Giles's Church, almost opposite, can be made if desired. Dating from between the thirteenth and fourteenth centuries, there are several interesting features which include a medieval monument to a lady, believed to be Margaret, wife of Henry de Ferrers and a number of remnants of Saxon crosses carved with interlaced knotwork.

When returning to your car, take the main road to the Market Square and head for the *Charles Cotton Hotel*, a large building which is plainly visible in the corner. When you are just beyond the *Devonshire Arms*, bear left on the Warslow road and the car park is on the right.

9

WALK 2

CAT & FIDDLE INN, WILDBOARCLOUGH AND THREE SHIRES HEAD.

This is a moderate walk which is predominantly over moorland terrain. It starts at the well-known *Cat and Fiddle Inn*, the second highest public house in England, and traverses Axe Edge Moor, a most uninviting place when conditions are bad. The first destination is Wildboarclough, once a thriving industrial community but now a sleepy picturesque hamlet and from there we make our way to Three Shires Head, the meeting point of three counties before returning once again over Axe Edge Moor to *The Cat and Fiddle*.

Map:
Ordnance Survey Outdoor Leisure Map 24

Start:
The Cat and Fiddle Inn.
Map reference SK 001 719.

Directions:
On the A537 road between Macclesfield and Buxton. Parking is available on the verge opposite the inn.

Distance:
Approximately 7 miles (12km).

Duration:
Four to four-and-a-half hours plus lunch break.

Refreshments:
Food is available at *The Crag Inn* at Wildboarclough and *The Cat and Fiddle Inn.*

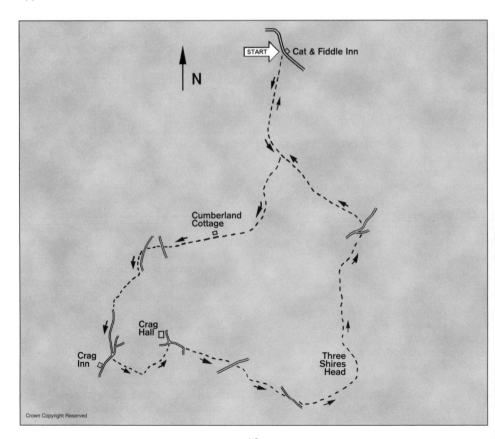

10

Setting out

The start of this walk could not be more obvious. The broad well-used footpath, once an ancient cartway, stretches away across Axe Edge Moor from right outside the front door of the inn. After approximately half-a-mile leave the relative ease of the smooth, even path behind and start to descend from the moor at a sign-post indicating Cumberland Cottage and Wildboarclough. The path follows Cumberland Clough, a deep rocky gully, for a further half-mile when it widens out into a narrow valley. Soon the path becomes less steep and a small building is passed on the right. This is Cumberland Cottage which is owned by the Scout Association and is often a temporary home to scouts engaged in weekend activities in the great outdoors. The path eventually emerges on a road by Clough House Farm.

Take the footpath opposite which passes by the farm and then crosses a footbridge to exit on yet another road. Cross this road and climb a ladder stile almost opposite to a footpath which rises slightly to the left and eventually becomes a metalled lane. Follow the lane up the hillside beside a plantation for a while and past a cottage on the right. Pass through a gate where it meets another lane and carry on straight ahead, now going downhill. As you walk along this lane brief views of the hamlet of Wildboarclough can be seen below through the trees on the left.

Wildboarclough

The name 'Wildboarclough' may well conjure up an image of an area where hordes of wild boar could be found and indeed boar were hunted here in the past, but not exclusively, so why the name? Well, when certain weather conditions prevail i.e. after a prolonged dry spell, the moors around become very dry and are unable to cope with sudden downpours. The result is that instead of soaking into the ground, the water rushes down from the hills and creates a tidal wave or 'bore' which floods the valley and causes much devastation.

Just such a freak occurrence happened during May of 1989 when many walls were washed away, bridges damaged and animals lost. There are records of a similar occurrence during 1932 and it is believed that it has happened on other, earlier occasions too, so it is thought that this may be the origin of the 'wild boar' in the name.

Wildboarclough is now a quiet, sleepy hamlet but in the mid-eighteenth century it was a thriving, bustling, industrial community. There used to be three large mills here, one of which could boast of machinery designed and built by a young James Brindley who later pioneered canal construction and went on to become the foremost engineer of his generation. Silk was the chief product at that time, employing a workforce of approximately six hundred but later the mills were converted to the manufacture of carpets. They were eventually demolished in 1958 leaving only the administration block which later became a sub-post office, the largest in the country. The large, imposing building that can be seen on the hillside opposite is Crag Hall, the country seat of Lord Derby.

When the lane meets a road, continue onwards in a south-westerly direction until you come to The Crag Inn on the right. This is an ideal spot for lunch, serving excellent food and walkers are always made welcome providing boots are removed before entering.

After leaving the inn, retrace your steps back along the road a little way until you come to a footpath on the right which crosses Clough Brook via a footbridge. Follow the path up through the trees by the side of a stream and then cross a stile into a meadow. The path is not very well defined here but continue straight ahead until a track is reached by Firs Farm. Turn left here and follow the track which eventually emerges on a road opposite Crag Hall.

Do not approach the Hall but turn right up the hill, and where the road begins to turn to the right, leave the road by a footpath which continues straight ahead through Leech Wood. Shortly, the path climbs out onto open moorland and crosses the A54 Congleton/Buxton road. It then traverses more moorland which, from time to time, can become quite wet and boggy. This does not persist for long however and soon a narrow road is reached by Cutthorn Farm. Pass the farm on the road and take the track on the left which skirts Cutthorn Hill, gradually descending to Three Shires Head.

Three Shires Head

As the name suggests this is the point at which three counties, Cheshire, Staffordshire and Derbyshire all meet. This was probably an extremely busy place in times gone by, with four packhorse routes meeting here, people would wait to hear the news from afar brought to them by the drovers or jaggermen. Trade between the Peak and the Cheshire Plain was prolific in those days and the traffic must have been quite heavy as one of the bridges has quite clearly been widened at some time.

Being a busy crossroads, as was common with all such places, there would probably have been a wayside pulpit where itinerant preachers, or even the jaggermen who tended to be very religious, would harangue those passing by much the same as they do at Hyde Park Corner today.

This spot has been significant to man throughout the ages and much superstition and speculation have grown about the place. There were three standing stones here at one time, testimony to the importance that was placed upon the location, but now these are no longer in evidence. It used to be said that the water could be used as a cure for witchcraft and other such things, this was probably due to the frequent reddish discolouration of the brook caused by various minerals contained in the surrounding hills.

Flash Money

The nearby village of Flash, the highest village in England, gained some notoriety due to its proximity to Three Shires Head. The ease with which one could escape the clutches of the law, simply by crossing from one county to another in those days, led to an influx of undesirables. Many of these were counterfeiters and consequently this was the origin of the term 'Flash Money'. Bare knuckle fights also took place here for the same reason. Do not cross the bridge, but carry on up the valley first climbing high above the river only to return to it further on where it is little more than a stream. Just below Holt Farm, turn left up the side of the valley to once again cross the A54 road.

Take the track which runs in a north-westerly direction almost opposite, it is an ancient cartway which crosses Axe Edge Moor. Follow it and eventually you will reach the sign-post for Cumberland Cottage and Wildboarclough where you passed earlier in the day. Carry on straight ahead retracing your steps until you arrive back at *The Cat and Fiddle Inn*.

The Cat and Fiddle Inn

The inn was built on the site of an old hunting lodge during the early eighteenth century by a banker from Macclesfield called John Ryle. Later he became the Mayor of Macclesfield and was subsequently elected as the first Member of Parliament for the Borough.

At 1690 feet, this is the second highest inn in England, the highest being at Tan Hill in North Yorkshire. The origin of the name is rather obscure, it has been attributed variously to Catherine le Fidele, the wife of Czar Peter the Great who was a close friend of the Duke of Devonshire, or to the Duke himself who is supposed to have enjoyed playing his fiddle there.

WALK 3

GRADBACH, DANEBRIDGE
AND THE DANE VALLEY

This is a walk with many interesting features. It covers some of the prettiest countryside along the Cheshire/Staffordshire border and takes in approximately five miles of the River Dane between Gradbach and Barleigh Ford Bridge. It is an easy walk which includes an eighteenth century mill, the site of a cottage where the occupants were forgers who murdered passing travellers for their possessions; and an ancient 'hollow way'. There is an abundance of birdlife in the woodland areas and deer can often be seen in the vicinity of Danebridge. In addition, the most vigilant walker may also be rewarded with the sighting of a wallaby.

Map:
Ordnance Survey Outdoor Leisure Map 24.

Start :
Gradbach Car Park. Map ref. SJ 999 662

Directions :
Leave the A54 by the Rose and Crown at Allgreave on a minor road sign-posted for Quarnford. After approximately two miles Manor Farm will be seen on the right and immediately after the farm make a reverse right hand turn into a lane marked 'Peter

Watson Scout Campsite'. The car park is on the right after a quarter-of-a-mile.

Distance :
The walk is approximately 11 miles (18.5km).

Duration :
Five hours plus lunch break.

Refreshments :
Meals can be had at
The Wild Boar Inn.

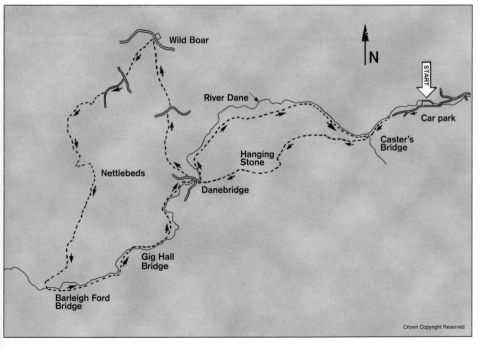

Crown Copyright Reserved

Setting out

Leave the car park and turn right up the lane. After a few minutes the entrance to Gradbach Mill Youth Hostel will be reached. Enter by the large gateposts on the right and walk down to the mill.

Gradbach Mill

The mill was originally built in 1640, although it is not known what its purpose was during the first 140 years. In 1780 it became a silk mill and was rebuilt in 1785 after the original was devastated by fire. The mill was highly successful over the next 100 years and was at the centre of a thriving community of over fifty cottages in the valley, all of which are now gone.

A striking feature of the mill was the water wheel which drove the machinery; said to have been the largest pocket water wheel in England its diameter was 38 feet and around its circumference were 96 pockets each with a capacity of 35 gallons. It was geared such that one turn of the main wheel resulted in 2500 revolutions of the drive shaft. Legend has it that a young girl once became trapped in the wheel and was crushed to death and forever after her cries could be heard every time the wheel turned.

In the late nineteenth century the mill was sold and converted into a sawmill and joiners shop providing timber for the Calke Abbey estate, near Derby. When this closed down the main population of the valley left to find employment elsewhere.

Opposite the mill stands Mill House and during the 1800s, when the last owners of the silk mill were both doctors, the extension built on the side was a surgery and consulting room. Before the last war, due to the popularity of the area, it became a cafe serving refreshments to the many visitors who flocked to the valley at weekends.

The Peter Watson Scout Camp Site

At the rear of Mill House is a stile, cross this into a field which is part of the Scout Camp site. The Peter Watson Scout Camp site was inaugurated in 1954. Its location amid such wild and scenic countryside makes it an ideal base for scouting activities and at weekends during the summer months the fields are populated with many campers from all parts of the UK and occasionally from even further afield. Follow the footpath straight ahead, then enter a track by a stile on the right. Walk along the track until it doubles back on itself, where you climb a step stile in a wall ahead of you. Turn right here and go downhill to Caster's (or Smelters) Bridge. The original bridge was a battlemented timber construction which was washed away in 1840. The name is derived from the presence of a forge nearby where counterfeit coinage is reputed to have been cast. There is an interesting tale relating to the forge.

Murder most foul

It is said that in the days when pedlars roamed the countryside selling their wares, one was passing by one evening and was offered a bed for the night. Whilst waiting for his supper he overheard a child's voice say "When will that old man be dead? I'm sure the oven is hot enough". Fearing for his life, the pedlar made his escape and went to the authorities. The militia rode out immediately and arrested the family and burnt the cottage down. It later transpired that they had made their living by waylaying lonely travellers and murdering them for their possessions, afterwards disposing of their bodies in the forge.

Wallabies

After crossing the bridge continue straight on up the hill, past the first sign-post indicating Danebridge, then turn right at the second in the direction of Swythamley. The footpath climbs steadily first to Castle Rocks and then, still heading for Swythamley, round the shoulder of the hill where it eventually meets another path joining from the left at a gate. The walk to this point through Forest Wood is unusual in that if you are lucky you could encounter a wallaby.

During the last war many animals were brought to Swythamley Hall from Whipsnade Zoo to escape the German bombs. When a fire broke out many of the animals escaped, including the wallabies. Most of them were recaptured with the exception of the wallabies and a pair of llamas. The llamas were unable to adapt to the conditions and died but the wallabies have survived to this day living in the woods above Gradbach. They are seen from time to time but they are extremely shy and such sightings are rare.

Hanging Stone

From the junction of the footpaths, climb the stile by the gate and continue straight ahead down a bridle road. The track descends first left, then right and then passes through a gate. Soon Hanging Stone can be seen on the right and where the track meets a crossroads carry on in the same direction through the gate. From here a detour can be made to the Hanging Stone if desired.

The stone is in fact a series of boulders stacked one above another and jutting out from the hillside. It is reputed to have been used for public hangings in the past although no evidence exists to support this. Local legend has it that the stone was also used for ritual sacrifices in ancient times. In 1934 a forester, whilst digging holes to plant new trees, found a hoard of gold, silver and copper coins beneath the stone.

There are two plaques on the stone, the first records the burial in 1874 of 'Burke', a dog belonging to the Swythamley Squire. The second plaque was erected in 1949 in memory of Lt. Col. Henry Courtney Brocklehurst, another Squire of Swythamley who was killed in active service in Burma in 1942. It later transpired that he had been taking part in a spying mission.

Danebridge

After visiting the stone, continue along the track until just beyond Hanging Stone Farm. Here a path leaves the track on the left, go over the stile in the wall and cross the field heading for a standing stone in the middle. Carry on past the stone and climb another stile in a fence on the right ahead and progress into a wood. This path descends steeply at first down a series of steps before passing through a quite delightful woodland setting. It eventually emerges down some more steps and over yet another stile into the Dane Valley. Turn left to the road and right across Dane Bridge.

Shortly after crossing the bridge take the path on the right, sign-posted 'The Wild Boar'. Go through the gate and head diagonally up the field and through another gate. The path now follows a straight line over a stile towards a gate by a farm. Pass through the gate, cross the road and through another gate. Head slightly right and cross another stile almost immediately. Cross the field diagonally right towards the trees, then keeping to the hedge on the right, walk to the bottom of the field and turn left. Cross a stile and the brook on the right, turn left over a wall and follow the path up the field to a gate by a bungalow.

Upon reaching the road turn right past Hammerton Farm and take the track through a gate on the left. Follow the track which eventually becomes a path and soon the A54 road and *The Wild Boar Inn* will be seen straight ahead.

The Wild Boar Inn

There are many places which make the claim that the last wild boar in England was killed there and this area is no exception. As the name suggests, nearby Wildboarclough is said to have been a particular haunt of the beasts but, like everywhere else, there is no evidence to support the claims. *The Wild Boar Inn* however, does have a somewhat unique relic, the skin of a wild boar hangs on the wall next to the bar and it wears spectacles! Whilst here the Inn can provide very good, reasonably priced food so this is a suitable place to stop for lunch, or a drink.

After leaving *The Wild Boar* take the right hand path opposite. Cross the brook and follow its course through the gully, eventually passing over a broken wall. The ground here is covered with the remains of many clays left by the Wild Boar Clay Pigeon Shooting Club. The gates from which they shoot can be seen on the hillside opposite.

Head diagonally right up the field and over a high wall at a ladder stile. Looking to the left from here you can see Hanging Stone and Forest Wood where you walked earlier. In the distance the rugged edge of the Roaches can also be seen. Continue on diagonally across the field to a stile in a fence, turn left and cross a stile over the wall. This brings you out onto the main Wincle road.

Greasley Hollow

Take the road opposite until two tracks appear on the right. Take the left hand track and then cross a stile on the left just before a farm. Keeping to the hedge on the left follow the path down into Greasley Hollow, a wooded valley. The path crosses the brook and then climbs high up the right hand side of the valley. When another brook is reached, cross it and climb over a broken stile turning sharp left up the field to a green track by Nettlebeds Farm.

When a sign-post is reached turn right over another stile. Keep to the hedge on the left, then cross a stile by a gate and bear diagonally right around the hill, eventually turning right at a gate to meet the Gritstone Trail which approaches from the right. Carry straight on along the Gritstone Trail following the waymarkers to Barleigh Ford Bridge. The path here is part of an old hollow way, an ancient sunken track, which was used by the Cistercian monks from Dieu la Cresse Abbey which was north of Leek, when travelling to and from their outpost at Wincle Grange.

The Dane Valley

After crossing Barleigh Ford Bridge follow the road until it turns sharp right over a bridge. Do not cross the bridge but continue straight ahead over a stile and along the towpath of what appears to be a small canal. This is in fact a supply or feeder channel which was constructed to take water from the River Dane at Gig Hall to top up Rudyard Reservoir which in turn was built to supply water to the Caldon Canal system.

Continue to follow the feeder until just before reaching what used to be the Feeder Keepers cottage, where a small glen can be seen on the right. Known as Meal-Ark Clough, during the Civil War the local folk are said to have hidden their cattle and horses here to keep them from the clutches of Oliver Cromwell's soldiers. A little further on, cross the Dane by Gig Hall Bridge and turn right. Notice the trout ladder by the weir, put there to help the fish get upstream. The path now follows the river through pasture-land to eventually emerge at the trout farm at Danebridge.

Turn right over the bridge and take the footpath on the left on which you arrived earlier. Instead of turning right up the steps continue straight ahead up the valley. The path passes through woodland where deer can sometimes be seen foraging. Still following the river, carry on through open moorland passing two modernised cottages on the way and eventually re-enter Forest Wood on a lower path than on the outward journey before once more arriving at Caster's Bridge.

Retracing your footsteps now, return through the Scout camp-site and Gradbach Mill and stopping at the gate to the mill look straight ahead to the skyline. This is Axe Edge Moor where the Dane rises just above Three Shires Head. It travels just twenty two miles before it eventually joins the River Weaver. Named after the Celtic Earth Goddess 'Dana' or 'Danu', it twists and turns through some of the most beautiful and varied countryside in the North West, and the five miles which have been followed on this walk bear testament to that. From here continue down the road and the car park is on the left.

16

WALK 4

THE HIGH PEAK AND TISSINGTON TRAILS

This walk takes in part of each of the above trails and since they were originally railway tracks, it is relatively undemanding. Built by canal engineers, they feature long flat stretches with only shallow inclines. Elsewhere on these lines there were extremely steep inclines where stationary steam engines were used to help haul the wagons up, but fortunately we do not encounter these on this route. In summer it is pure delight to walk the trails because of the profusion of wild flowers which grow alongside the tracks. The views from the embankments also lend interest to the walk. Between the trails the route takes in a number of places of interest including an excavated Roman farmhouse and the remains of a fourteenth century Cistercian Grange.

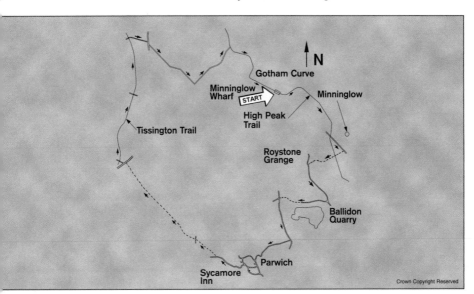

Crown Copyright Reserved

Map:
Ordnance Survey Outdoor Leisure Map 24.

Start:
Minninglow Wharf car park
Map Reference SK 194 583.

Directions:
Minninglow Wharf is three-quarters of a mile south of Pikehall which is situated on the A5012 between Newhaven and Grangemill.

Distance:
Approximately 12 miles (19km).

Duration:
Approximately 5 hours plus lunch.

Refreshments:
The *Sycamore* pub at Parwich.

The High Peak Trail

Minninglow Wharf was a station on the Cromford and High Peak Railway. Like all of the stations on this line it was called a 'wharf' because the line was originally designed early in the nineteenth century as a canal. The intention was to link two existing canals, the Peak Forest Canal at Whaley Bridge and the Cromford Canal in the south. The project was abandoned however, due to major engineering problems and a lack of water.

As a railway it formed an important part of the canal system until 1853, but then the development of other railways took away much of the freight from the canals and it was relegated to being only a local line. It finally closed in 1962 when it was converted into *The High Peak Trail* for the benefit of walkers, riders and cyclists.

Minning Low

From the car park go south along the trail and notice the large embankment, testimony to the skills of the engineers of the time. Over on the left, the tree-capped hill is Minning Low, a stone age 'barrow' or burial site. It lies on the route of a prehistoric thoroughfare which connected Minning Low with other burial sites at Arbor Low and Harborough Rocks. Later, the Romans improved the track and incorporated it into their road known as the Street between *Aqua Arnemetiae* (Buxton) and Little Chester (Derby). The barrow contained at least four tombs constructed of stone slabs which formed a chamber with a further large slab supported on the top as a roof. Its chamber was plundered many years ago but it is believed to have contained at least one skeleton. All around the site large quantities of Roman artefacts have been found suggesting that this was a significant stopping place for travellers in those days.

Carry on following the trail until you eventually reach an old quarry where the remains of a crane and rails from a narrow gauge tramway can be seen. Moving on, the trail crosses another embankment and in the field on the left hand side, a tunnel-like structure is an old lime kiln where lime was produced for agricultural use. Limestone and coal were put in at the top and it was left to burn for a few days before being extracted from the bottom.

Continuing past the lime kiln, the way is eventually barred by two large gates where the High Peak Trail is intersected by the Roystone Grange Trail, the first archaeological trail to be opened in Britain. Just beyond the gates on the right are the remains of an old kiln where once firebricks were made from the unusual silica sand deposits which are to be found here in a band about five miles wide between Parsley Hay and Brassington. Return to the Roystone Grange Trail and turn right towards Minning Low. This wide green track, now called Gallowlow Lane, was at one time part of an old drovers road which went to Wirksworth from Cheshire via Leek, Hartington and Biggin. After a short while climb a stile in the wall on the right by a footpath sign and head down the field towards a stone arch which carries the High Peak Trail over the footpath. As you cross the field you will pass a mere, a circular pond especially created to catch dew. In this area where the underlying rock is predominantly limestone, any surface water tends to soak into the ground very quickly which makes watering livestock rather difficult for farmers. A mere was the solution to the problem and long ago they were made by digging a circular depression and lining it with puddled clay. Men used to specialise in their construction and were in great demand travelling far and wide plying their trade.

Go under the arch and follow the obvious path down the valley to Roystone Grange. As you do so you may wonder about the unusual building with a curved roof high on the hillside to the right. This was once an explosives store for the nearby quarries sited in this remote spot for safety.

Roystone Grange

Cross the stile at the bottom of the valley and turn right up the farm approach road. Go through the gate and the farmyard and just beyond on the left look out for an old barn where an interpretive notice has been attached.

This valley represents an important archaeological site in that a Roman farming community lived here for about 300 years. Settling here at around 200 AD, they were totally self-sufficient, growing their crops and grazing their animals in the surrounding fields. Just above the barn a farmstead has been excavated, it had low walls and a thatched roof was supported by timber posts. At least four other similar farmsteads were sited nearby a little to the south. After viewing the site return to the track and retrace your steps through the farmyard and past the stile where you joined the road. A little ahead on the right stands a small building in a walled enclosure. Go through a gate and walk to the right of the building.

Look carefully and although overgrown, the remains of some walls can be seen. This is the original Roystone Grange, a medieval monastic sheep farm which belonged to the white-robed Cistercian monks from Garendon Abbey in Leicestershire. Occupied between

1100 and 1300 AD the monks originally called the grange 'Revestones', they grazed their sheep throughout the valley and exported the wool as far away as Italy. An interpretive signboard is attached to the wall of the adjacent building. This building in itself is of some interest. It was a pump house containing a large water-cooled engine which pumped compressed air through cast-iron pipes to drive the rock drills used in the nearby quarries during the 1800s.

Rejoin the road and walk south down the valley towards Ballidon Quarry. Look out for a sign-post pointing to a gate on the right hand side of the lane. Go through the gate, and follow the track through the quarry. Before long the track becomes a footpath winding its way along the bottom of a small valley. When a plantation appears on the top of the left side of the valley, be prepared to turn off, up the hill and head for a stile by a gate at a road beyond the trees.

Parwich

Turn left, down the road until a narrow, tree-lined lane is reached on the right. Take this lane and eventually you will find yourself in the quiet, picturesque village of Parwich. Once there, head in the direction of the church, go past the village green and the *Sycamore* pub is on the left opposite the village pond. It is known from flints which have been unearthed in the area that Parwich, or the land in the immediate vicinity, has been occupied since prehistoric times. The first documentary evidence of its existence however, appears in the year 966 when the village was granted a Royal Charter. There are a great many types and styles of cottage lining the narrow streets and reflecting the various occupations, from sheep farming to lead mining and quarrying, all of which have contributed to the prosperity of the village over the years.

Upon leaving the village, take the road to Alsop-en-le-Dale. The road initially has a number of blind bends so beware of the traffic. After a short uphill stretch, look out for some farm buildings on the left of the road and just beyond you will find a sign-post on the right indicating a footpath which heads diagonally across the fields to Middlehill Barn. Continue to follow the path across the approach road to Middlehill Farm and onwards into Eaton Dale. A gradual climb up this wide, dry dale bypasses Eatondale Wood and Oxdales Farm before meeting the A515 Ashbourne/Newhaven road by a disused quarry.

The Tissington Trail

Cross the road carefully and turn left before taking a right turn down a minor road towards a large bridge over which the Tissington Trail passes. Join the trail at the bridge and head north. Like the High Peak Trail, the Tissington Trail is also a disused railway line. In this case the line ran between Ashbourne and Buxton and eventually closed in 1934.

This section of the trail is virtually flat and affords good views towards Cheshire in the west. It is lined with a myriad of wild flowers which are particularly beautiful in the summer. Continue to follow the trail until the Biggin road is reached at the second bridge. Leave the trail here and go right, away from Biggin village to the junction with the A515. Cross the road carefully and take a green track almost opposite to the right.

This is once again the old drovers road upon which you walked earlier but this stretch is known as Cardlemere Lane and was first recorded in 1276. Follow the lane for almost a mile and then turn left where a gate bars the way. This is now Green Lane, a medieval road which ran between Alsop-en-le-Dale and Pikehall and which now meanders between fields until it eventually meets the High Peak Trail.

Gotham Curve

Turn right here and follow the trail down a shallow gradient to a very sharp left hand bend. This is Gotham Curve, when the railway was still in use it was reputed to be the tightest curve on any railway in the country. With a radius of only 165 feet (50m) and turning through almost ninety degrees it must have been quite an experience to travel on this route. Carry on along the trail through pleasant woodland and shortly you will be back at the car park at Minninglow Wharf.

WALK 5

LATHKILL DALE

This walk takes in one of the most beautiful dales in England. Although Lathkill Dale has seen lead mining since Roman times, much of what remains has been mellowed by the relentless encroachment of nature and now blends with and adds to the splendour of the scenery. The river rises in a cave amidst the limestone tors at the upper reaches of the dale. It tumbles down the dale and sometimes disappears beneath the ground altogether before it becomes shallower and wider and an abundance of trout can be seen swimming lazily amongst the weeds. Much of the dale is now a nature reserve and the managed woodland supports a great deal of wildlife.

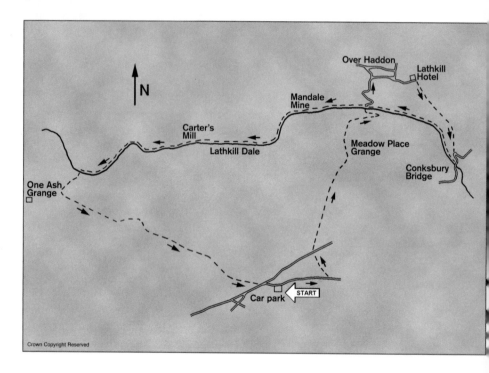

Map:
Ordnance Survey Outdoor Leisure Map 24.

Start:
Car park and picnic area - Moor Lane.
Map reference SK 194 645.

Directions:
Leave the A515 at Parsley Hay in the direction of Monyash. Take the first right for Youlgreave and continue for approximately three miles. At the sign indicating 'Picnic Area' fork right and the car park is on the right.

Distance:
The walk is a little over 7 miles approximately 11.75km.

Duration:
Three to three-and-a-half hours plus lunch break.

Refreshments:
Food can be obtained at *The Lathkill Hotel* at Over Haddon.

Setting out

From the car park turn right up the lane. After approximately half-a-mile cross a stile on the left and proceed straight ahead to another stile at the edge of a narrow stand of trees. These trees mark the location of Long Rake, an old mine-working site which stretches from here as far as the well-known megalithic stone circle at Arbor Low.

The miners of old, having found what they sought, in this case lead, would follow the seam along the surface digging only to a safe depth and leaving behind them a great scar or 'rake'. Mining is still taking place a little further to the west but nowadays the product is calcite and fluorspar.

Meadow Place Grange

Pass through the rake and make for another stile in a wall across the field. Carefully cross the road and another stile immediately opposite to join a footpath which goes half right across the meadow. Passing over two stiles, follow the guide-posts to Meadow Place Grange. As the name 'Grange' suggests this was once a sheep farming outpost for a monastic order. This was, and still is an area where the land is suitable for little else but grazing, and consequently sheep farming has predominated here for many years.

Meadow Place Grange belonged to Leicester Abbey and is one of three local farms which were once owned by religious orders during the middle ages. The footpath takes us through the Grange and across the court to leave by another gate almost opposite the entrance.

The path now leads slightly right across the meadow to meet a gate and track which descends through a nature reserve into Lathkill Dale. Follow the track down through the woods to the footbridge at Lathkill Lodge. Cross the bridge and follow the road uphill to the village of Over Haddon.

Over Haddon

Until the middle of the fourteenth century, there were two Haddons but during the course of building Haddon Hall the village of Nether Haddon was demolished leaving just the chapel which was incorporated into the hall. Now the 'Over' in Over Haddon is the only reminder that its partner ever existed. The village had a brief period of fame during the seventeenth century when a girl named Martha Taylor suddenly stopped eating at the age of sixteen. For eighteen months, while villagers and local physicians kept constant watch, she apparently ate nothing and suffered no ill effects. Word of the phenomenon spread far and wide and four books were eventually written about her. Little is known about her later life other than that she lived normally for many years after her fast.

The Lathkill Hotel

Carry on up the road and turn right immediately after the church. Note the height of the doorways on some of the older cottages on this road; people tend to be much taller now than in days gone by. At the end of the road follow the signs for *The Lathkill Hotel*, a suitable place to stop for lunch.

From the hotel pass through the stile in the corner of the wall outside. Follow the well-defined path which descends gradually over the meadow, crossing a double stile at a wall and eventually another at a fence.

The path now follows the lip of the dale giving fine views all around. Cross a further double stile at a wall and where the path forks, bear right and down to a gap in the wall where the path meets a road and a right turn takes you to Conksbury Bridge. This was once a packhorse bridge on an ancient saltway. Do not cross the river but turn through the gate on the right before the bridge onto a path which follows the river Lathkill through the dale.

Lathkill Dale

Lathkill is Scandinavian in origin, a clear sign that the Vikings settled in this area. The word means 'narrow valley with a barn' and was first recorded in 1280 as Lathegyll.

There are several man-made weirs along this stretch of the river. These were built to maintain the water level for the trout during drier weather when the river sometimes disappears underground altogether. The river emerges from a cave at the head of the dale near Monyash and is reputed to be the purest in Britain and the fish can easily be seen in its clear waters.

There are many varieties of birds here including coots, grebes, moorhens and mallards. Dippers can be seen throughout the year and in summer the grey wagtail is a common sight. You may also be lucky enough to see a kingfisher feeding by the banks.

The path continues to follow the river until Lathkill Lodge is reached once again. Here turn right up the hill but then turn immediately left beside Sour Mill which is about four hundred and seventy years old and was worked until the early nineteenth century. You have now rejoined the river footpath and are back in the peace and quiet of the nature reserve but it was not always so idyllic. From as early as Roman times this area has been involved in the mining of lead. There are several small tunnels on the right of the path. These were exploration shafts and may be unsafe, therefore the temptation to enter them should be resisted.

In 1854 there was a mini gold rush in the dale when it was thought that gold had been found in one of the disused mine workings. A company was founded and many people speculated only to lose everything when it was discovered two years later to be nothing more than iron pyrites or 'fools gold'.

The Mandale Mine

On the left, running alongside the river, is a narrow channel or sough. By far the biggest problem that faced the miners in those early days was that of flooding. This was overcome by excavating small tunnels laterally into the various levels of the mine from which the water would drain and be channelled away via the soughs.

This one is over a mile long and took twenty-three years to construct. It belonged to the Mandale Mine, reputed to be one of the oldest lead mines in Derbyshire, having been worked from the thirteenth century and possibly earlier. At the point where it disappears under a stone arch, a path on the right climbs up the hill to the remains of the old pumping house and the entrance to the mine. The pump house once housed a beam engine which is now in the care of the Peak District Mines Historical Society. Once again these old workings can be extremely dangerous and the utmost care should be taken.

From the pumping house take the path which runs parallel with the river alongside which there is evidence of another earlier attempt at draining the mine. This involved the use of a pump driven by a water wheel. The water was diverted from higher up the dale and crossed the river via an aqueduct, the remains of which will be seen later. From there it flowed along the gully on the right of the path, over the wheel and away via the sough.

Follow the path down to the river. From this point onwards there are many signs of early mining activity. Concrete posts are laid horizontally to cover disused shafts and evidence of excavation can be seen on both sides of the path. All of these sites are potentially dangerous and should be avoided. The ash woodlands in this part of the dale have been managed from the eleventh century and attract many species of birdlife. Chaffinches, robins, wrens and tits can be spotted and you may also be lucky enough to see a woodpecker or little owl. Several species of bat are also found here.

Carry on following the river footpath until a stile is reached where the river passes over a weir. This was the site of Carter's Mill, a corn mill dating from the early nineteenth century, of which there is now no trace apart from two millstones lying beside the path. The mill was still there in the thirties but the iron water wheel was removed during the last war.

Parson's Tor

Continue to follow the river for a further 800 yards to the footbridge at the junction with Cales Dale. On the right is Parson's Tor, so named after a one-time Rector of Monyash. According to legend, on October 12th 1776, the Reverend Robert Lomas who was well known for his drinking, died at this spot. Returning in the snow from a day's 'preaching' at Bakewell, he mounted his horse in a drunken state and set forth for home. Upon reaching the edge of the limestone tor his horse halted but he urged it on. Instead it threw him and he fell to his death. A ballad was published in 1864 telling the tale.

Turn left here and cross the bridge. This was at one time a sheepwash bridge where the farmers of old would wash their sheep in the river to remove parasites and stop the spread of disease. Follow the footpath up the hill into Cales Dale and when it splits, take the left hand fork down to the bottom of the valley. Cross the stile and climb the other side by a series of 120 steep steps.

At the top there is a kissing gate in a wall and it is worth stopping here for a moment not only to regain one's breath but also for the view over the dale. Looking straight across Cales Dale a farm, One Ash Grange, can be seen on the opposite side. Like Meadow Place Grange, this was also once inhabited by monks. It belonged to Roche Abbey, a Cistercian monastery founded in 1147 near Maltby in Yorkshire, as did nearby Calling Low Farm which we pass shortly. The Abbey used the Grange as a penal colony and sent penitent monks here to ponder on their shortcomings. Later, the Grange belonged to a Quaker family who made some structural alterations in 1747 and later still John Bright, the Quaker leader, brought his new bride to spend their honeymoon there.

The Limestone Way

The route now follows the 'Limestone Way' a well-marked footpath across meadows to Calling Low Farm, the third of the monastic outposts. The path no longer passes through the farm but has been diverted to the left of the buildings, it is however well defined and easy to follow. Having walked around the farm pick up the original path which continues in more or less a straight line across the fields until a stile is reached in a wall by a roadside. Turn left up the road and right at the fork, the car park is approximately 300 yards on the right.

Lathkill Dale and its nature reserve are managed by English Nature. The beauty of the dale and the wide variety of wildlife which it sustains is entirely due to their hard work. Please ensure that you help them by always following the Country Code.

It must be emphasised that mining has taken place in this area since Roman times and has left a legacy of some 50,000 mineshafts many of which are now overgrown and hidden from sight. The golden rule is therefore,

"always keep to the footpath",

better safe than sorry!

23

WALK 6

LYME PARK CIRCULAR

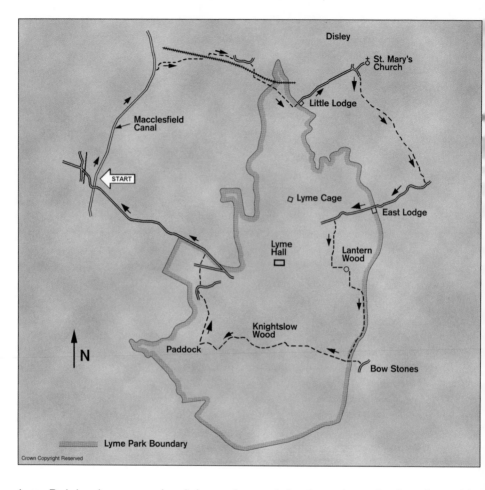

Lyme Park has been an enclosed deer park since the thirteenth century. In 1346 the Black Prince, heir to the throne, was saved from death by Piers Legh at the battle of Crecy and the King, Edward III rewarded his gallantry by granting him the estate. It remained the home of the Legh family for over six hundred years. It is now administered by the National Trust and is still a deer park covering some 1300 acres. The present hall was rebuilt in the classical Palladian style during the eighteenth century to replace an earlier Tudor and Jacobean building of 1578 although there are records of a hall standing here as early as 1456. This walk encircles the park weaving in and out of its boundaries. The estate is criss-crossed with many footpaths and it is possible to shorten, or indeed lengthen the walk at numerous points around the circuit. A diversion to visit the hall and gardens is well worth the effort if you wish to do so.

Map:
Ordnance Survey Sheet SJ 88/89 Stockport (South).

Start:
Vernon Mount car park, Higher Poynton.

Directions:

From the A523 Stockport/Macclesfield road at Poynton, take the road sign-posted for Pott Shrigley (Park Lane). After half-a-mile fork left at Middlewood Road and first right at Anson Road. Continue across the junction, past *The Boars Head* and the car park is situated on the left.

Distance:

A little over 8 miles, approximately 13.25 km.

Duration:

Approximately 5 hours including lunch.

Refreshments:

A packed lunch will be required on this walk.

Poynton Village

Poynton village grew with the coal industry which flourished here for many years until the coal became too expensive to extract. The last mine closed in the thirties but, although not conspicuous, there is still much evidence remaining to testify to the seventy four pits that were worked here. The car park where you are parked was the site of the Nelson Pit and until quite recently was little more than the remains of a slag heap. From the car park, join the canal towpath and turn left. The canal was opened in 1831 and was principally used for the transportation of coal. After passing under a bridge, look out for a wood on a small hill on the left. At the far end, where a path joins the canal, was the site of Lower Canal Pit which was known locally as 'Old Redlegs'. This was because of the original pumping engine which had two red painted legs working over the shaft. This engine was destroyed when the engine house burned down in the late 1800s. Upper Canal Pit was situated opposite on the other bank of the canal though no evidence remains.

The Ladybrook Valley Trail

Continue to walk along the towpath until just beyond bridge No.13 where you leave the left bank of the canal by a gate on the left. Turn back upon yourself and cross the bridge to join the right hand canal bank. In a hundred yards or so, the canal crosses a valley via a steep embankment and just before it does so a stile

bars the way. Do not cross the stile but descend by a path on the right immediately in front of it to a timber footbridge. You are now on the 'Ladybrook Valley Trail' and the way forward is clearly indicated by waymarkers.

After crossing the footbridge, climb a stile and make your way across the meadow, roughly following the river. When you come to a footbridge cross it, and turning right, head for a ladder stile a little further up the valley. Climb the stile into a lane and then another almost opposite. The path now climbs the railway embankment and crosses the lines. Great care must be taken here, look both ways and listen carefully for approaching trains. When you are certain that it is safe to do so, cross the lines quickly and take the path opposite.

Keep to the right and follow the lower path to cross a footbridge and a stile, before passing through a farm gate at a lane. Turn right past the farm and follow the lane until it turns left over a bridge, here leave the lane and rejoin the trail by a stile on the right. Cross the field and go under the railway arch turning left as soon as you do so. Walk straight down the field alongside the railway embankment and upon reaching the wall at the far end, go left over the footbridge and climb the ladder stile over the wall, leaving the trail and entering Lyme Park.

Lyme Park

The name 'Lyme' originates from the ancient forest of Lyme which covered four counties and stretched from Ashton-under-Lyne in the north to Newcastle under Lyme in the south. At one time this entire area was covered with trees and Lyme Forest formed the eastern boundary of the Royal hunting ground which included Macclesfield Forest among others. Curiously the name Lyme does not derive from the Lime tree but rather the Elm.

The path now continues straight ahead passing Brookside Cottage on the right. The smart exterior suggests a building of quite recent date but it was in fact built in the late seventeenth century and was a smithy for a time in the 1800s. Take care crossing the main drive to the hall and head for the gate opposite. The cottage beside the gate is Red Lane Lodge or 'Little Lodge' as it used to be known because in the park's heyday it was only a single storey building. This gate was used by the Legh family when they visited St. Mary's Church at Disley; it was also the gate used by the park employees because they were not allowed to use the main gate. Leave the park by this gate and walk up Red Lane until you reach the point where it bends to the left. Turn right here along a track and, if desired, in a few yards a detour to the left can be made to visit the church. The original church was built by the fifth Sir Piers Legh who was both a knight and a priest. The family still maintains an interest in the church today and there are several memorials to them, both in the church and in the churchyard.

A Gallon of Beer a Day!

An interesting memorial, which can be found in the central aisle of the church, is that of Joseph Watson a one-time keeper at the park. Joseph Watson was something of a character, famed for his prowess in driving deer. He is reputed to have won a bet for his master, the Squire Legh, by driving twenty four stags, alone from Lyme to Windsor Forest, a quite remarkable achievement. He is also supposed to have drunk a gallon of beer every day of his working life at Lyme. If this is true it certainly did him no harm, since he lived to the age of 104. His tombstone reads:-

"Here lyeth Interred the body of Joseph Watson, Buried June 3rd, 1753, aged 104 years. He was Park Keeper at Lyme more than 64 years, and was ye first that Perfected the Art of Driving ye Stags. Reader, take notice, the Longest life is short. Here also lyeth the Body of Elizabeth, his wife, aged 94 years, to whom he had been married 74 years."

Lyme Cage

Returning to the track, turn left into Green Lane and continue straight ahead. Soon fine views open up to your right, dominated by the somewhat curious Lyme Cage. Built about the same time as the church, it was designed to be lived in and indeed, park employees were housed there until the nineteen-twenties, using oil lamps and drawing water from the nearby stream. As the name suggests it was probably also used as a place of temporary detention for law breakers whilst they waited for transportation to the court of Macclesfield Hundred. It is also suggested that it might have been used as a vantage point from which the ladies would watch the menfolk take part in the hunt. Continue up the lane and at Higher Stoneridge Farm, carry on straight ahead where the lane becomes a track and then a footpath. Cross a stile and ford a small stream before bearing right to another stile which gives access to a lane. Turn right and follow the lane to Bollinhurst Bridge, then start the gradual ascent up to East Lodge where you re-enter the park. As you walk along the track look over to your right where you may see a herd of Red Deer which often congregates in this area of the park.

Lantern Wood

Just beyond a small copse on the left, take the second stile and walk up the hill with the boundary walls of first Keepers Wood and then Lantern Wood on your right. Upon reaching a ladder stile, climb over the wall into Lantern Wood. On entering the wood, walk straight ahead through the trees and shortly a clearing will appear on the right at the top of which is the Lantern tower, after which the wood is named. Walk down to the tower for a closer look. It was once part of the original Elizabethan hall and was rebuilt here in 1729 as a folly. Look down the clearing now for a good view of the present hall. After a short stop return past the tower and continue to the right on the original footpath. Follow the path through the wood and upon reaching the boundary wall, climb the ladder stile and turn left up the hill, passing a small disused quarry on the right. This is one of many such quarries in the vicinity which used to provide sandstone for the various buildings in the park. Continue on up the hill, following the wall and bear right at the top. In a little while a small, round stone panoramic viewing point will be reached. On it there is an engraved brass plaque which indicates all of the significant landmarks on the horizon. On a clear day one can see as far as the Welsh hills from here.

Bowstones

Carry on following the wall until Bowstones Cottage is reached on the left where it is worth a small detour to see the 'Bowstones'. Climb the ladder stile and then a further stile to emerge at a narrow road. The site of the 'Bowstones' is on the left, just beyond the cottage gate. The popular theory, which gives rise to the name, is that there were originally three standing stones, around which yew rods were placed and left to season, after which they were ideal for making longbows. A more probable explanation however, is that the stones are the broken shafts of Celtic crosses which were often used as waymarkers or boundary stones on the highways of the day and this would have been an important crossroads at the time. Runic symbols carved into the edges of the stones would seem to support this. The crossheads are missing but there are some at Lyme Hall which it is thought could have originally belonged to these shafts. Nearby, two gravestones were discovered commemorating victims of an early outbreak of the plague. Although primitive, they were carved with the following lines:-

"John Hampson and his wife
and three children left this life,
                              1646."
and:-

"Think it not strange our bones lie here,
Thine may lie thou know'st not where
                              Elizabeth Hampson."

Unfortunately, the stones were removed to an unknown place some time ago.

The 'White Lady'

Return over the stiles and continuing straight ahead, make your way across the moor and down to Knightslow Wood. Cross the ladder stile by the gate and once into the wood turn immediately left. The name 'Knightslow' is a reference to the legend that the second Sir Piers Legh was buried here after being mortally wounded at the Battle of Agincourt in 1415. He apparently started for home but only got as far as Paris where he died, after which his body was returned to Lyme and buried on the hill in the wood. It is said that an apparition, the 'White Lady', supposedly the distraught ghost of either his wife or daughter, still haunts the park forever mourning and searching for his grave. When you reach the far edge of the wood, climb the ladder stile and take the lower, left hand path. Walk alongside the wall with Cluse Hey, a steep-sided gorge formed by

Poynton Brook, on the left. Shortly after making a right turn, go left away from the wall and make your way up to Paddock Cottage. The cottage dates from the seventeenth century and was lived in by park employees until as recently as 1932. It consisted of only two rooms, one above the other, and the inhabitants used candles or oil lamps, and had to fetch water from the brook in the valley below. It was derelict until quite recently but it has now been completely renovated and restored to its original condition. If you look East over Cluse Hey from here, you may see a herd of Red Deer which often spends the winter on this moor.

Turn North and walk along the edge of Pursefield Wood until at the end of the ridge, just before a large patch of Rhododendrons, the path descends to the left to meet a gate in the valley below. Pass through the gate and walk through the small car park, before taking a path on the left marked by two small wooden posts. Walk over rough grass meadow and cross an estate road before taking a narrow path immediately opposite, alongside a fence. Turn left when the next estate road is reached and eventually leave the park for the last time by a kissing gate at Windgather Cottage.

Continue downhill on the lane, past Haresteads Farm and eventually, Elm Wood Nature Reserve on the left. This land, once ravaged by coal mining activities, has been allowed to revert to its natural state in the hope that the wildlife will return once again.

A little further on, as you approach the canal once more, a large expanse of water will be seen on the left. This is known locally as 'Wide Hole' and was not as might be thought, constructed deliberately as part of the canal, but appeared suddenly in about 1870 as a result of mining subsidence. Cross the canal bridge and join the canal towpath, turning left.

As you cross the towpath bridge look to your left at the boatyard. This was a wharf built to enable coal to be loaded from the Nelson Pit onto narrow boats. The boats themselves were assembled in a pool on the opposite side of the canal where there was also a boatbuilder's shop and repair facility. Having crossed the bridge, the car park entrance is on the left a few yards further on.

WALK 7

MONSAL HEAD AND SEVEN DALES

The scenery in the southern Peak District is arguably the most attractive in the National Park. Personally I find a certain peace and tranquillity in the dales that is not to be found elsewhere. This is a walk that takes in seven such dales all of which are slightly different and each with a character of its own. The industrial history of the Litton and Cressbrook mills in Tideswell Dale and Cressbrook Dale, contrast with the beauty of Upperdale and Monsal Dale. The towering Ravens Buttress also in Cressbrook Dale where stone age man once lived and Tansley Dale where fossils abound in the discarded mining waste. This walk has a variety of interesting features and should appeal to everyone.

Map:
Ordnance Survey Outdoor Leisure Map 24.

Start:
Tideswell Dale car park and picnic area. Map reference SK 154 742.

Directions:
From Tideswell drive south on the B6049, the car park is approximately one mile on the left.

Distance:
The walk is approximately 8 miles (13km)

Duration:
Four to four-and-a-half hours plus lunch break.

Refreshments:
Meals can be obtained at the *Monsal Head Hotel* at Monsal Head.

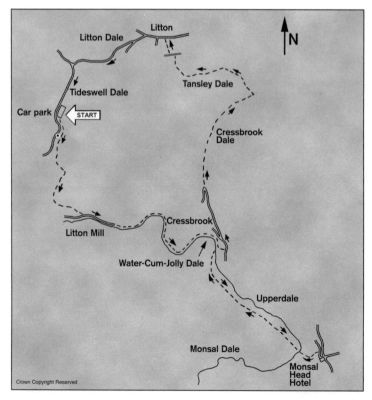

Tidi's Well

From the car park take the track beside the toilets and proceed down Tideswell Dale. The dale, like the village, is named after an eighth century Saxon king called Tidi and a spring which was located on his land hereabouts hence 'Tidi's well' which eventually became Tideswell. When the track forks take the right hand path which continues down the dale and then once again fork right over a footbridge at the next junction. Shortly before the path emerges at the road, Tideswell Dale

Cave can be seen on the left. The cave is about 100 foot long with a small chamber at the end. Turn left down the road following the River Wye for approximately 200 yards until Litton Mill is reached.

The 'Devil's Mill'

The original mill was built in 1782 by Ellis Needham of Haregate Hall near Tideswell with his partner Thomas Frith, a farmer. The mill was to be used for cotton spinning with machinery powered by water wheels. The arrival of such mills usually signalled an improvement in the fortunes of those lucky enough to gain employment so, as with mills elsewhere, a small community soon grew up beside it.

This however, was not to be one of the happiest places to work. In its early years the mill had a reputation for the inhumane treatment of its child workforce. The children were orphans and street urchins brought from London with the promise of a better, healthier life. Unfortunately the reality was to be the exact opposite. The regime was extremely hard with long hours and little or no concern for the health of the workers. Punishment for alleged wrongdoing was cruel to say the least and included such things as the filing of teeth, spitting in the mouths and being beaten with sticks whilst hanging from the ceiling in cages. The death rate was so high that in order to avoid suspicion bodies were taken away and buried in churchyards elsewhere such as Tideswell and Taddington.

The conditions were improved dramatically in the mid-nineteenth century however when one of the apprentices spoke out about the cruelty. A novel, 'The Devil's Mill' was inspired by the experiences of the children who lived and worked here and it did much to help in the cause of child labour at the time. Nowadays it is thought the book was nothing more than melodramatic propaganda designed to accelerate the passing of the Factories Act in 1833.

The route now passes through the mill buildings on a concessionary footpath which eventually bears right to join the river bank. This part of the walk, through Miller's Dale, is particularly attractive during spring and early summer when many species of duck and wildfowl can be seen bobbing on the river. Follow the riverside footpath until you arrive at the romantically named Water-cum-Jolly Dale, a legacy of the Victorian age. As you enter the dale the river begins to widen and forms a large mill pond. The path skirts the pond under rather impressive overhanging limestone cliffs where rock climbers are frequently found. It then crosses the mill leat and enters the grounds of Cressbrook Mill. Cross the river by the bridge on the right and climb the hillside to the left to join the Monsal Trail in Upperdale.

The Monsal Trail

The Monsal Trail follows the route of the old Buxton to Bakewell railway line. Built in the 1860s, the railway revolutionised life for the local people but not everyone was impressed by the new technology. The author and art critic, John Ruskin said, 'The valley is gone and with it the Gods, now every fool in Buxton can be at Bakewell in half-an-hour and every fool at Bakewell in Buxton; which you think a lucrative process of change you fools everywhere'.

Clearly Ruskin objected to the desecration of the idyllic surroundings but he need not have worried too much. The tunnels and the viaduct which so enraged him have blended into the landscape and the viaduct is now seen as a picturesque landmark. The line eventually closed down in 1968 but a group of railway enthusiasts still entertains hopes that it can be re-opened as a tourist attraction.

Follow the trail until the viaduct is reached at the junction with Monsal Dale. Continue over the viaduct and just before the tunnel take the footpath on the left which climbs the valley side up to Monsal Head. This is a very popular spot with trippers because there are fine views of both Upperdale and Monsal Dale from here. The *Monsal Head Hotel* serves very good food and there is a cafe nearby, therefore this makes an ideal lunch stop.

After lunch the early part of the afternoon's walk is simply to retrace your steps along the Monsal Trail. When the point is reached where the footpath leaves the old railway line there is a bench and an information board relating to

Cressbrook Mill which can be seen to advantage from here.

Cressbrook Mill

Built in 1815, this imposing Georgian structure is now sadly dilapidated. It is an elegant building, superbly proportioned and is visually quite attractive. On the roof the bellcote, which was used to summon the workforce, is an unusually ornate feature. The Peak Park Planning Board had searched in vain for an investor to save the building and for a long time it seemed unlikely to happen, however at the time of writing there are some signs of restoration. It was used as a cotton mill for one hundred and fifty years until it closed in 1965. The present building replaced an earlier one built by Richard Arkwright in 1779.

In the early years, like Litton Mill, child labour was used here too although conditions were considerably better, but beatings and punishment were still the order of the day. Later, children were well looked after and even had their own accommodation, being housed in Dale Terrace, a row of cottages originally known as Apprentices Row to the north of the mill. The first manager at the mill was the so-called 'Derbyshire Minstrel', William Newton.

Follow the footpath down the hillside and across the river again to the mill yard. Pass through the mill grounds and behind the mill itself; the full extent of the dereliction can be seen from here. As you pass through the gates onto the road a pond will be seen over the wall opposite. This was the mill pond of the earlier mill which was powered by the Cress Brook. Cress still grows in the brook and in the past it was harvested for sale. Lilies of the Valley were another crop that was picked in the woods and sold at the market in Manchester. Turn left outside the gates and at the fork in the road bear left to visit the village. The church of St. John was built in 1903 and was the first church in the village. Previously the locals had held religious meetings in each others homes. In the late eighteenth century there was apparently a factory here which made bicycles with wooden wheels and also a peppermint distillery which used wild mint gathered from the woods.

In the mid-nineteenth century a farmer digging a hole for a gatepost nearby, unearthed a skeleton still wearing full Cavalier uniform and complete with weapons. The story goes that in 1651 during the Civil War, a battle took place at Hartington and the Royalist commander who was fatally wounded was brought here by his supporters and subsequently buried in the woods when he died.

After leaving the village take the Litton road you were on earlier and walk up the hill beneath a canopy of trees into Cressbrook Dale. At the top of the hill, where the road turns sharp left, continue straight ahead into the woods on a clearly-defined path.

Ravenscliffe Cave

As you emerge from the woods the majestic sight of Ravens Buttress, rising to a height of 150ft., can be seen amongst the limestone cliffs on the opposite side of the dale. Cressbrook Dale at this point is sometimes called Ravensdale due to the large population of Ravens that inhabited the buttress until the middle of the last century. Unfortunately their reputation of being birds of ill omen caused them to be hunted down and they eventually died out altogether. In the 'Old Stone Age', more than 5000 years ago, palaeolithic man lived here in nearby Ravenscliffe Cave where flint tools and other artefacts have been found together with bones of bear, reindeer and rhinoceros dating from that period.

The path now proceeds over a grassy hillside and then descends to the bottom of the dale to cross the Cress Brook by way of a stile and footbridge. Continue walking along the valley bottom until a fork in the path is reached. At this point bear right and climb up high above the trees towards the lip of the dale where a fine panoramic view is to be had.

From this point on, the way forward is clear descending and following the valley side round to the left. The dale is dry here and the footpath runs along the bottom through piles of rock and shale. Together with the occasional adit, a short horizontal shaft dug into the hillside, these bear testimony to the extensive lead mining which took place in these parts in the past.

he limestone, from which the 'White Peak' derives its name, is the oldest rock in the district and was formed in the carboniferous period 330 million years ago from the shells of sea creatures. You can see the evidence of this quite easily in the shape of fossils which can be found amongst the discarded rock piles.

Murder most Foul

Soon, Tansley Dale comes into view joining from the left and is entered via a stile in the wall below, however, a little further on, a large limestone outcrop stands out prominently at the head of Cressbrook Dale, high up on the right hand side. This is known as Peter's Stone and it attained some considerable notoriety in 1815 when a gibbet was erected upon it and the body of a murderer was publicly displayed there. The crime had taken place at nearby Wardlow Mires when a 21 year old man, Anthony Lingard from Tideswell, killed the old woman who was in charge of the toll bar whilst attempting to steal a pair of shoes. He was caught and subsequently tried and hung at Derby but afterwards his body was returned to the scene of the crime for public display as an example to other potential wrongdoers. The case aroused so much interest that crowds of people flocked from near and far to see him and the local people, seeing an opportunity to make a little money, erected stalls in and around the spot to cater for their needs. Before long travelling entertainers had arrived and the event turned into a fair. The spectacle lasted for many days and caused much consternation amongst the local gentry. Subsequently questions were asked in parliament, the outcome of which was the passing of various reforms which resulted in this being the last gibbeting to take place in England.

is said that the ghost of the murderer still haunts this spot and on occasions, walkers who have stopped to sit and eat their lunch here, have claimed to have experienced the strange sensation of an invisible pair of hands round their necks, trying to strangle them. Perhaps he prefers boots nowadays. You have been warned!

Litton

Head up Tansley Dale, and at the top climb a stile and head diagonally right to the corner of a wall. Cross to the opposite corner of the field where another stile leads to a farm track. Turn left and in a few yards on the right climb a further stile before once again crossing the field to the opposite corner where a final stile brings you out in the village of Litton.

Litton, which means 'farm on the hill', is typical of many of the small villages in the Peak where most of the property, both farms and cottages, have grown up beside a turnpike. The result is a long narrow development from the village green backed by long narrow walled fields, probably a legacy of the medieval strip farming system. Although the walls came later they almost certainly predate the eighteenth century Enclosures Act.

Litton was the birthplace of William Bagshawe, the non-conformist minister who became known as 'The Apostle of the Peak'. Otherwise there is nothing particularly remarkable about Litton, but it does have a nice feeling of spaciousness unlike many other Derbyshire villages where the cottages seem to crowd in upon one another. There is one cottage, on the left when you join the road, which dates from 1639 but much of the remaining buildings were built around the early eighteenth century.

Turn left and walk through the village, notice the old stocks standing on the green outside the *Red Lion* pub. Follow the road round to the left, sign-posted to 'Tideswell and Millers Dale'. This road passes down through Litton Dale to a T-junction with the B6049. As you walk down the road take a look at the long narrow fields on the right which illustrate perfectly the early practice of strip farming. When you reach the junction you are once again in Tideswell Dale having visited seven dales altogether throughout the day. Cross the road to the paved footpath opposite and walk left, down the hill. After walking for approximately half-a-mile, re-cross the road to take a footpath which runs beside a row of mature beech trees and which eventually leads straight into the car park from which you started.

WALK 8

SHINING TOR, GOYT VALLEY AND ERRWOOD HALL.

This is a walk of contrasts taking in a high level ridge, moorland, forestry and a picturesque valley. When the weather is favourable there are some superb views from the summit of Shining Tor. It is a fairly easy walk with a short steepish ascent initially and a long shallow, steady climb at the end. Interesting features include Shining Tor, Errwood Reservoir, the ruins of Victorian Errwood Hall and an unusual shrine dedicated to the memory of a Spanish lady.

Maps:
Ordnance Survey Outdoor Leisure Map 24.
Ordnance Survey Tourist Map 4.

Start:
Pym Chair car park. Map ref. SJ 995 768.

Directions:
From Kettleshulme village take the sign posted road for Goyt valley. The car park is on the left after approximately two miles.

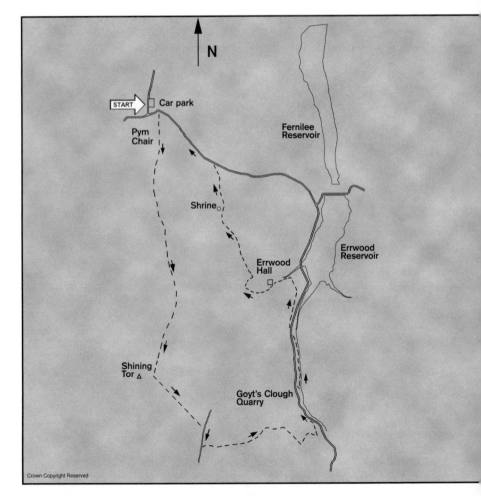

Distance:
The walk is approximately 7 miles (11.25km)

Duration:
Four-and-a-half to five-and-a-half hours including a generous stop for lunch and time to investigate the remains of the Hall and the shrine.

Refreshments:
A packed lunch is recommended on this walk.

Setting out

Upon leaving the car park, turn left and walk to the T-junction. Turn left again along the road and in approximately 150 yards, take the footpath on the right which is sign-posted for Shining Tor.

Pym Chair

Initially the path rises steeply to Pym Chair, where once a natural chair-shaped rock stood. Its name, according to legend, is derived from a number of different sources the most popular of which seems to be that of a highwayman called Pym who used to lie in wait for unsuspecting travellers amongst the rocks here because of the clear view along all three roads. It is also said that a preacher named Pym used to meet here in secret with his followers. That they had to meet in secret and in such an isolated spot suggests that whatever he preached must have been illegal or forbidden and the area has long been vaguely associated with evil, maybe as a result of this story. The rock 'chair' itself is alleged to have been broken up mysteriously one night around the turn of the century because of its links with the Devil.

The likeliest explanation however is that 'Pym' is derived from the Celtic words pim, pin or pen which mean 'a lofty position' and that the 'chair' was a chair-like rock which has subsequently been broken up to provide hardcore during repairs to the road.

Shortly the path becomes a pleasant ridge walk which traverses firstly Cats Tor and then The Tors before reaching Shining Tor. It is possible that some sort of conflict occurred here in the distant past as 'Cat' is thought to be derived from the Celtic word cat or cath, which meant 'place of great battle'.

Shining Tor

On clear days there are good views to be seen to both East and West along this part of the walk. When you reach the point where the wall on your right turns sharp left, cross the stile to the Ordnance Survey triangulation pillar which marks the summit of Shining Tor.

Originally these pillars, or 'Trig Points', were used by the Ordnance Survey in the making of maps. By taking sightings of various geographical features from these fixed points it is possible to locate them and measure their height in relation to one another. Until quite recently all maps were produced in this way but with the advent of satellites it is now possible to make the necessary calculations with much more accuracy from photographs taken whilst orbiting the earth.

As a result of this change many of the triangulation pillars will no longer be maintained by the Ordnance Survey. This has upset the walking fraternity who have for many years used them as navigational aids and waymarkers. Now due to numerous protests the Ordnance Survey are proposing to offer some of them for adoption by groups or individuals who will undertake the responsibility for their continued upkeep.

Shining Tor, at 1834ft. above sea level, is the highest point in the vicinity and as such affords some fine views. To the northwest the buildings of both Stockport and Manchester can be seen and looking west, below is the vast expanse of the Cheshire Plain with the radio telescope at Jodrell Bank and the Berwyn Mountains in the distance. Turning south, the distinctive shape of Shutlingsloe (the Cheshire Matterhorn) can be seen on the horizon.

The Cat and Fiddle Inn

Having enjoyed the view return back over the stile and, keeping the wall on your right continue on the footpath across the moor. Upon reaching a stile, cross over it and bear right to another stile by a gate. Cross this one too and go straight ahead along the track. In front of you a radio mast can be seen with a building nearby. This is *The Cat and Fiddle Inn*, at 1690ft. the second highest pub in England.

After approximately fifty yards take the footpath which descends steadily to the left. This path eventually takes you to Stake Clough, a narrow valley with a small brook running through it. Cross the brook and take the footpath which runs alongside the plantation on the left. Your route now follows a 'ride' or fire gap through the plantation and the spruce and larch trees make a pleasant contrast from the featureless moorland of the previous footpaths. The path eventually drops into Deep Clough, crosses a footbridge and bears to the left, once again entering the plantation. The ruined buildings on the right are what is left of a factory which over a hundred years ago used to crush and bag barytes for use in the paint-making industry.

Goyt Valley

When a stile is reached at a track turn left, parallel with the road through the Goyt Valley. The name was first recorded in 1244 as 'Guit' and probably originates from 'Gota', which means watercourse. On the right, below the road is Goyt's Bridge, a three hundred year old packhorse bridge which originally stood further north but was dismantled and rebuilt here when the valley was flooded to form Errwood reservoir. Shortly, as you walk down the track you will come to a disused quarry at Goyt's Clough where a picnic area has been established. This makes an ideal place to stop for lunch.

In 1670 a certain Thomas Pickford was contracted to supply paving slabs from this quarry to London. He ran a team of fifty packhorses to transport the slabs the two hundred or so miles to London and returned empty until one day he realised that he could make a little extra profit bringing goods back to Derbyshire. Soon afterwards the famous haulage company of that name was born.

Having eaten your lunch, leave the quarry and continue down the valley by way of the road. After passing the 'No Entry' signs and before reaching the bridge, look out for a path on the right which descends via a series of steps to the brook. Follow the bank of the brook rising gently on a wide track, until it joins once again with the road. Take the gated track opposite which is sign-posted for Errwood Hall. The trees here are predominantly Scots Pine, the only native species of Britain which are still commercially grown. They are easily recognised by their single-sided growth and lack of low-level branches.

Soon the reservoir appears ahead and there are fine views of the opposite bank where the old road that served the valley can clearly be traced winding round the shoulder of the hill. The creation of the reservoir has brought life of a different kind to the valley now in the shape of the yachting club which is located on the far side nearer to the dam. This is a popular spot and during the summer months many different craft can be seen sailing here. Errwood was constructed in 1967 and holds 937 million gallons of water. It was the second of two reservoirs built here to serve the Stockport area, the first being Fernilee a little further north, which was completed in 1938 and holds 1087 million gallons.

Before the flooding of the valley there was quite a large population either living or working here. The valley gave its name to a breed of sheep, the 'Dale o' Goyt' which eventually became known as 'Derbyshire Gritstones'. Besides having fifteen farms there was Chilworth Mill, a gunpowder factory which supplied the local quarries and is said to have provided the gunpowder for use against the Spanish Armada in 1588. During the Great War the demand was such that it employed 120 men working seven days a week. In earlier times there was a paint factory employing 22 men near Goyt's Clough and even a coal mine belonging to Errwood Hall which was situated at the southern end of the valley.

Errwood Hall

The track you are now walking along was originally the main approach road to Errwood Hall. It is not hard to imagine the rigours of travel in those days when all transport was by either carriage or cart and the only metalled oads were the turnpikes. Upon reaching the junction turn left and follow the wide well-made track as it meanders through the many shrubs and specimen trees that were planted here to enhance the Hall's environment. The rhododendrons were brought back as ballast in the hull of the yacht 'Marquita' when it returned empty from voyages abroad with its owner, the builder of Errwood Hall. It must have been quite idyllic before the rhododendrons took over. Continue on this track until you come to some steps on the right. Climb these and turn right until you reach the ruins of the Hall.

Once an elegant Victorian mansion, the Hall was finally demolished in 1934. It was built in 1830 by Samuel Grimshawe, a rich industrialist and was occupied by his family for over a hundred years until the last member died. The Hall was then purchased by Stockport Corporation and became a Youth Hostel for a short time. Soon after this the NWWB were successful in gaining permission to build the reservoirs and amid fears of pollution, the Hall was eventually pulled down. As can be seen the Hall was quite extensive, at one time employing as many as twenty servants. The Grimshawes took an active part in the thriving farming community of the valley even to the extent of providing a small school within the Hall for the benefit of the local children as well as their own.

The family were devout Catholics and evidence of this can still be seen at the burial ground. Take the footpath across the remains of the garden to the left of the Hall. Climb the steps and proceed along the path for approximately 100 yards. The burial ground is situated at the top of the hill on the righthand side. Should you not wish to climb the hill the burial ground can be bypassed by continuing along the path through the trees until the junction with a path approaching from the right is reached by a wall. If intending to visit the graves take the path up a short flight of steps on the right and follow the trail up the hill bearing left as you go. The burial ground will be seen straight ahead surrounded by railings. As you enter by the gate, you will see that many people have been buried here. There

must have been an excellent relationship between the 'masters' and their staff because not only were the family laid to rest here but also their servants and even the captain of their yacht who gave thirty years' service to the Grimshawes.

Upon leaving the burial ground turn left at the gate and descend the hill until you reach the junction with the earlier path. Your way now takes you through the gap in the wall and then to the right. Follow the path down and to the right where eventually a series of steps with a handrail lead you to a footbridge. Water tends to flow along the path and down the steps here and although it is not normally a major problem, care should be taken in winter when it can be treacherous if it freezes.

Miss Dolores Shrine

Having crossed the bridge turn left and begin the gradual climb up Foxlow Edge keeping the brook on your left. After a while a small circular stone building will be seen ahead. Built by the Grimshawe family, this is a shrine erected in memory of Miss Dolores de Bergrin, a Spanish lady who was both friend and companion to Mrs. Grimshawe. She was also governess to the children and occasional teacher at the school in the Hall. She died, somewhat ironically, whilst returning from a pilgrimage to Lourdes in 1889.

From the shrine, return to the path and continue the climb up the valley and soon a road will be seen ahead. Known as 'the street', this was at one time part of a Roman road which connected Bramhall in Cheshire with Buxton, passing through Adlington, Pott Shrigley and the Goyt Valley. Later, during medieval times it became one of the principal routes upon which valuable salt was transported into the Peak from the Cheshire Plain and wool was carried in the opposite direction.

When the road is reached, cross over carefully and turn left up the hill. The path follows the road to the crest of the hill at Pym Chair where the walk started and a right turn at the junction will return you to the car park which is on your right.

WALK 9

WILDBOARCLOUGH, MACCLESFIELD FOREST AND SHUTLINGSLOE

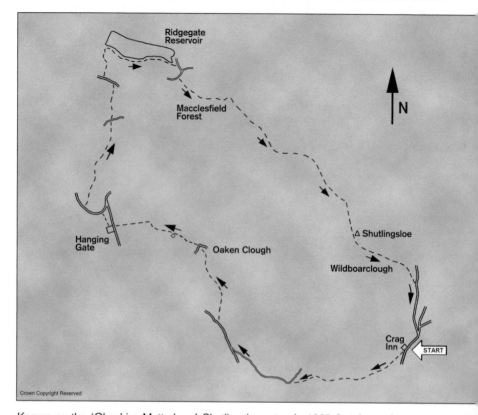

Crown Copyright Reserved

Known as the 'Cheshire Matterhorn' Shutlingsloe, at only 1660 feet is not by any means the highest peak in the area, but is a distinctive landmark that can be seen for many miles around. This walk starts in Wildboarclough to the east of Shutlingsloe and circles the peak in a clockwise direction eventually reaching the picturesque reservoirs at Langley on the edge of Macclesfield forest. From there the route takes you through the forest and up and over the peak to sample the splendid views from the top. This is not a strenuous walk but it rises steadily from the very start and continues to do so until the descent from the summit, however the views are worth the effort.

Map:
Ordnance Survey Outdoor Leisure Map 24

Start:
Either in the hamlet of Wildboarclough opposite the bridge Map Reference SJ 983 687 or at the *Crag Inn* at Map Reference SJ 981 685.

Directions:
Wildboarclough is situated on a minor road between the A54 Buxton/Congleton road to

the south and the A537 Buxton/Macclesfield road to the north.

Distance:
Approximately 7 miles (11 km).

Duration:
Approximately 5 hours including lunch.

Refreshments:
A meal can be obtained at the *Hanging Gate Inn* at the approximate half-way stage.

Setting out

Walk south down the road from Wildboarclough and just beyond the *Crag Inn* climb a stile over the wall on the right. The footpath rises up across the fields passing through a group of small hawthorn trees and then follows the contours of the hill offering good views over Clough Brook Valley to the left. Carry on via a number of stiles until the path takes you diagonally right to cross a small brook just below Higher Nab Farm. Walk up to the top right hand corner of the field and go through a gate before climbing a stile in the wall on the right. You are now on a farm track and a left turn will lead you to a road.

Follow the road and when you reach a junction continue forward until just beyond the gate to Heron Crag on the left. At this point take the footpath on the right which follows the bank of the stream and eventually crosses it by a stone footbridge. Walk up Oaken Clough and where the path forks at a small ruined building go to the right and pass below Oaken Clough Farm as you near the top. Cross the farm access road and ascend the hill on the left by a green track which terminates in a stile. The path now goes diagonally right across rough pasture and passes a small tarn on the left before reaching another stile. Turn left over the stile and walk between walls on a path which emerges on a road opposite the *Hanging Gate Inn*.

Ritual Sacrifice

This is an ideal place for a break or lunch, the inn provides good food and affords splendid views across the valley to Croker Hill or Sutton Common as it has come to be known. This is the hill across the valley with the large telecommunications tower on the top. It has the reputation of having been a Beltane Hill in Celtic times, a hill that had special Druidic significance and was used for ceremonial and sacrificial purposes. On the eve of the solstice or 'Beltane', fires would be lit and flaming bales of hay would be rolled from the top of the hill to the valley below in celebration of the changing of the seasons. The inn was first recorded in 1668 but is undoubtedly much older. In the sixteen hundreds it was known simply as the 'Gate' but this had a rather more ominous meaning to that which we might suppose today. The word gate is derived from the Viking word 'gata' which means, 'entrance to' or 'way to' thus Hanging Gate probably refers to a pointer to the place where hangings took place. There is however no evidence of where the gallows may have been sited.

The Gritstone Trail

After lunch take a short footpath which leads via the pub yard to a road below. Turn left here and walk down the road for approximately one hundred yards where it is intersected by the Gritstone Trail. Go right, over the stile and follow the trail, by the distinctive footprint and 'G' waymarkers, over fields and through the yard of a large farm. Continue to follow the waymarkers to the right of the farm buildings and at a junction with a lane take the stile almost opposite.

Carry on straight ahead over more fields to pass Greenbarn, another farm, and then bear left along the farm approach road and cross a stile on the right immediately after a cottage. The path bends round behind the cottage and joins a lane where you turn left and in a few paces leave the lane to go right over a stile into a wood.

Macclesfield Forest

The path now takes you by way of a footbridge, through the wood and via a series of steps, over the hill to emerge above Ridgegate Reservoir where a right turn is indicated by a sign-post reading 'Shutlingsloe'. The way forward now follows 'Forest Trail No. 3' which proceeds via wide, though sometimes muddy, well-defined tracks through Macclesfield Forest.

The forest is administered by North West Water and provides drinking water for Macclesfield from Ridgegate and Trentabank reservoirs. Although predominantly coniferous now, the forest still retains many indigenous trees, a relic of the ancient Royal hunting forest which stretched for many miles in the past. It is home to a great many species of birdlife and keen ornithologists may feel that it is worth a further visit for this alone.

As the trail climbs higher the trees begin to thin out and occasional glimpses of the bare expanse of hillside above the forest may be seen. Soon you leave the forest by a path on the right and climb a short hill at the top of which is bleak, open moorland where sheep grazing is the only viable use.

Ahead lies an obvious footpath across the peat and heather. Much restoration work has taken place here, evidence of which is the large stone slabs, flown in by helicopter and laid end-to-end to replace what had become an almost perpetual quagmire. Such is the popularity of this route that the erosion caused by the constant streams of boots passing this way had grown to alarming proportions and action had to be taken. Fortunately it was decided that reclamation was better than closure and, providing the weather is kind, you can now cross with relatively dry feet.

Shutlingsloe

Once you have crossed the moor the path brings you to the foot of the Shutlingsloe peak. A short, steep climb by way of a series of newly-built stone steps completes the ascent and at 1659 feet above sea level you are rewarded with a superb panoramic view from the triangulation point on the summit. A plaque has been attached to a rock to assist in identification of the various landmarks that can be seen from here.

The descent is via a tricky, boulder-strewn path on the eastern side of the hill and care should be taken to keep your feet. It soon becomes less steep however and as the going gets gradually easier one can look around and enjoy the view once more. The large grand-looking building across the valley is Crag Hall, the country seat of the Lords Derby.

Wildboarclough

The path now passes to the right of Shutlingsloe Farm before meeting a lane at right angles. Turn right along the lane and keeping a plantation to your left, look through the trees where occasional glimpses of the hamlet of Wildboarclough can be seen.

Now a quiet, sleepy place, it is hard to imagine that this was once a thriving industrial community. There were three silk mills here employing some six hundred people. Amongst them was a young man called James Brindley who, at that time, was employed as a millwright, maintaining and repairing the machinery. In later life however, despite being illiterate, he was destined to become famous as a pioneer of canal building and the foremost civil engineer of his generation.

The name "Wildboarclough" conjures up an image of an area where hordes of wild boar could be found and indeed boar were hunted here in the past, but no more so than anywhere else, so why the name? When certain weather conditions prevail i.e. after a prolonged dry spell, the moors around become very dry and are unable to cope with sudden downpours. The result is that instead of soaking into the ground, the water rushes down from the hills and creates a tidal wave or 'bore' which floods the valley and causes much devastation.

Just such a freak happening occurred during May of 1989 when many walls were washed away and bridges damaged. Fortunately no human lives were lost but numerous sheep and cattle were carried away by the torrent only to be found many miles away downstream. This is commemorated by a plaque attached to the parapet of the bridge in the centre of the hamlet. There are records of a similar occurrence in 1932 and it is believed that it has happened on other, earlier, occasions too. It seems that this valley is particularly prone to such floods and therefore this may well be the origin of the 'wild boar' in the name.

Continue on down the lane until at the junction with the road, turn left for Wildboarclough or right for the *Crag Inn*.

WALK 10

CHEE DALE AND THE MONSAL TRAIL.

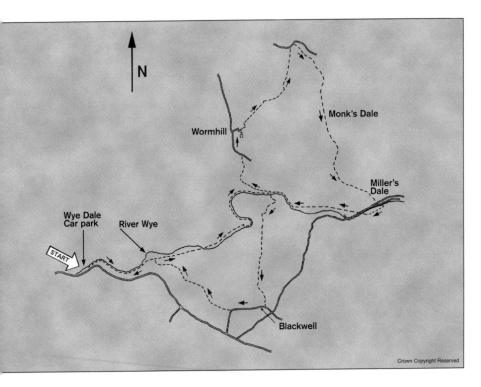

Crown Copyright Reserved

This is a route which would perhaps be best attempted at a time when there has been little or no rain. Being the only true gorge in the Peak, the walk along the River Wye is quite an experience, however, negotiating the stepping stones and steep banks can be difficult during rain or when the river is high. Please do not allow this to put you off because the walk through Chee Dale, initially along part of the Monsal Trail, is well worth the effort. The remainder of the route, whilst not as dramatic, is equally scenic. The village of Wormhill, where the well-known civil engineer James Brindley spent his early years, is visited followed by Monk's Dale and the nature reserve. We then rejoin the Monsal Trail at Miller's Dale before climbing out of the Wye valley, via the site of a Celtic settlement, in the direction of Blackwell completing the walk in the fields above rather than in Chee Dale itself.

Map:
Ordnance Survey Outdoor Leisure Map 24.

Start:
Wye Dale car park on the Buxton/Bakewell road. Map Ref. SK 104 726.

Directions:
Take the A6 from Buxton in the direction of Bakewell and the car park is situated on the left opposite Topley Pike Quarry.

Distance:
Approximately 8-and-a-half miles (14km).

Duration:
Approximately 5 hours including lunch.

Refreshments:
A Tea Room in Wormhill, or the *Angler's Rest* at Miller's Dale.

The Monsal Trail

From the far end of the car park take the riverside track and walk to the third viaduct where a series of steps leads up to the Monsal Trail. This is the trackbed of the disused railway from Miller's Dale to Buxton. It was a branch line from the London/Manchester main line which was first opened by the Midland Railway in 1863. It became extremely busy for a time but after the Second World War traffic gradually declined until the rationalisation of the railway network in 1962 brought it to an end. The section of line through the Peak finally closed in 1968.

A group of railway enthusiasts apparently still have ambitions to re-open the line as a tourist attraction but it is highly unlikely that they will ever be able to meet the cost of maintaining the tunnels. At the moment however, the Peak National Park authority have purchased the trackbed and opened it up to visitors. There is no doubting that it provides excellent walking and riding in some of the most scenic countryside in the Park and attracts a great many people to the area.

Chee Dale

Turn right along the trail and shortly the junction with the main line will be reached, its route clearly visible on the left. You are now entering Chee Dale and the views on both sides of the trail are quite breathtaking, firstly with Plum Buttress on the right followed by the dramatically steep rock faces that make the Dale so popular with climbers. Having passed through two short tunnels eventually the blocked entrance of Chee Tor tunnel is reached and the way forward now is by way of a footpath on the right which descends to the river's edge via a footbridge. At this point you continue on in the same direction but the ease of the trail has been left behind. The river passes through a gorge and when the banks come to an end progress is made via forty-four stepping stones beside the overhanging cliffs where climbers are often to be found. Beyond the stepping stones the dale is wider but not

by a great deal and the path demands some agility in clambering up and down the rocky and thickly wooded bank, sometimes balancing precariously above the river. Eventually, the going becomes less strenuous and two small footbridges are crossed at Wormhill Springs where, after particularly heavy rain, water is supposed to gush from the ground in a number of different places before flowing into the river. Gradually the dale opens up as you reach a sign-post at a footbridge. The way to the right, over the bridge, goes to Blackwell and the river path straight ahead leads to Miller's Dale but for the moment you should turn to the left and make your way up the side of the dale in the direction of Wormhill. The path climbs steadily back along the dale side before turning away towards Wormhill, eventually meeting a road at right angles beside a cottage. Turn left here and walk towards the centre of the village.

Wormhill

The name Wormhill is popularly thought to be derived from 'Wolfhill' in the belief that this was a particular stronghold of the wolf in the White Peak. Certainly in medieval times when the village helped administer the Royal Forest of the Peak, many of the men of the village had duties in the forest in return for owning strips of land. Some of these duties included the hunting and killing of wolves. In 1324, it was recorded that a land-holder named John de Wolfhunt was responsible for the 'taking of wolves' from the Peak Forest at certain times of the year. Despite its age, the village does not have a great many old buildings. The Hall, on the right of the road, was built in 1697 and is quite attractive but most of the rest of the village, was built during the nineteenth century. Wormhill does however have a minor claim to fame. The famous civil engineer James Brindley who became the foremost pioneer of canal building was born at Tunstead, a nearby hamlet in 1716. In his early years he lived and worked at Manor House Farm and a memorial has been erected over a natural spring in the centre of the village adjacent to the old stocks.

Before departing the village you may wish to take some refreshment at one of the Tea Rooms. When you are ready to move on make your way along the main road through the village and then head for the church. The church is not particularly old, it was built about 1864 but it does have an interesting tower and spire. From outside the church take the footpath which continues straight ahead beside a house, then pass through an iron gate into a field, before heading straight up towards a distant sign-post. Cross the next small field to join a wide, walled green track.

Eventually the track becomes a tree-lined path which is a little rough underfoot but has excellent views in all directions. Follow this ancient path between gnarled old trees for approximately a quarter-of-a-mile finally descending to meet the old coaching road between Wormhill and Tideswell.

Monk's Dale

The road crosses the valley separating two dales, Peter Dale on the left and Monk's Dale on the right. The dales are connected by a footpath which crosses the road at about the centre and here you turn right into Monk's Dale. The dale is at first wide and grassy but soon you pass between high banks which signal the start of a nature reserve. The path here is overgrown and rough and progress can be slow but the wild state of the surroundings is of course the ideal habitat for the many creatures and plants which are being encouraged. Should you prefer a path with a little more comfort there is an alternative route which follows the Limestone Way along the high ground on the left of the dale before joining the lower path close to Miller's Dale.

Monk's Dale, as one might guess, derives its name from its former religious associations. About seven hundred years ago a grange and chapel were sited here belonging to the Lenton Cluniacs, a powerful monastic order whose abbey was near to Nottingham. In those days behaviour was very different from that which

we might expect today and the monks here had a reputation for high living. There were frequent disputes with the Dean of Lichfield over land ownership and occasionally deputations were sent to Rome for the Pope himself to pass judgement.

The 'Brothers' were not averse to resorting to violence either when settling a disagreement. One story tells of an occasion when the Dean of Lichfield's men stole some sheep and hid them in the church at nearby Tideswell. The monks broke into the church to retrieve the sheep and seriously wounded the clergy in the process. All that remains to show where the grange and chapel once stood is a series of grassy hillocks and ridges.

As you near the end of the dale the trees gradually give way to open grass hillsides and soon the path crosses a stile and emerges down a short flight of steps beside the small church into Miller's Dale.

Miller's Dale

Previously called Millhouse Dale, Miller's Dale probably became known by that name because it once had two mills on the River Wye. A water wheel can still be seen opposite the *Angler's Rest* pub, this belonged to the Tideswell Mill and the wood-turning centre was the Wormhill Mill which dated from the twelfth century allthough it was rebuilt in 1860. The hamlet, once a quiet backwater, became a bustling centre of activity following the construction of the new Midland Railway. Buxton has always been renowned for its spa waters but in Victorian times it was particularly popular and it became fashionable to travel from miles around to take 'the cure'. When the branch line was constructed to accommodate the constant flow of visitors, Miller's Dale was transformed into a busy cosmopolitan junction almost overnight. Cross the road, being careful of the traffic, and turn down the road for Litton Mills. The *Angler's Rest* is on the left if you require lunch but otherwise immediately turn right to cross a footbridge over the Wye. Once over, start the gradual ascent up the hillside to join the Monsal Trail once more. Turn right and shortly you will come across a sign on the left indicating 'Lime kilns' where a short detour can be made if desired.

Lime Kilns

About three hundred million years ago this whole area was covered by a warm shallow sea and when it receded the limestone was formed during the carboniferous period from the shells and skeletons of numerous sea creatures that lived in the vicinity. These lime kilns were built in the nineteenth century as a commercial venture. Small kilns had been producing quicklime for agricultural use for many years but with increasing demands from industry and with the abundance of limestone available from local quarries it made sense to produce it on a larger scale. The quicklime was produced by burning limestone together with coal and this was tipped into the kiln from above whilst the fire was tended and the lime recovered from the flues at the bottom.

The last of the kilns, situated further along the trail beyond Miller's Dale station, was closed in 1944. This one remained in use throughout the Second World War when the glow from the tops had to be shielded from the night skies in case enemy bombers used them to navigate by and therefore locate their intended targets more easily.

Miller's Dale Station

After viewing the kilns continue along the trail and soon you will come across the double viaduct which signals your arrival at Miller's Dale station. The reason for the two bridges is that when the Buxton branch line was constructed the original proved to be inadequate for the volume of traffic. The station of course no longer serves its original purpose but one can see from the area of the site that for a small country hamlet it was an unusually substantial facility having five platforms in 1904. Freight as well as the passenger traffic formed a significant part of the daily schedule here. There were milk churns collected from the surrounding farms to be sent to London and of course the quicklime to be distributed to the chemical industry all over the country. In return, large quantities of coal were unloaded for use in the nearby lime kilns. Only one platform now remains but the station hosts the Ranger Service and an information centre, there is also a large car park and public toilets making it a popular base for visitors. A little way beyond the station, on the right of the trail, the more recent lime kilns referred to earlier can be found. These are in a better state of repair and may give a better understanding of how they were used.

Continue along the trail until you reach a viaduct where you descend to the bank of the Wye once more by a path on the right immediately before it. Having reached the river bank turn right and in a short while you will arrive at the footbridge where you climbed up to Wormhill earlier. Turn left over the bridge and as you do so look down into the clear waters where you will see Brown Trout of all sizes lazily swimming up and down and feeding on the occasional unsuspecting insect.

Celtic settlement

From the bridge follow the path which proceeds initially diagonally left and then turns right and climbs steeply up the hillside. This area was once the site of a Celtic settlement and the small stone enclosures seen on the lower slopes were built by them. At the top of the hill it is worth stopping for a moment to get your breath back and to appreciate the magnificent view over Chee Dale. It is possible to trace where you have walked from Wormhill towards Monk's Dale and then Miller's Dale over to the right.

Having climbed the hill you can now proceed across the fields with relative ease. Cross the first two walls by stiles and then head for a gate in the far right of the next field which leads to a track that, after an initial turn to the left, goes straight to Blackwell Hall Farm. Pass through the farmyard and follow the lane down to a minor road where a right turn takes you to the hamlet of Blackwell.

Blackwell

There is evidence of very early farming in the Blackwell area, probably from before the Saxons. Also, as was seen earlier, the Celts made their home here. As in so many areas in the White Peak the motivation to settle here was the ease with which water could be obtained close to the surface of the ground. Its presence is due to the underlying igneous rock which, being non-porous holds the water within the porous limestone above and this gives rise to the frequency with which 'well' appears in local place names. In 1559, Bess of Hardwick became the owner of the manor of Blackwell and intended to build a grand house here. Although plans were drawn the project did not develop beyond this stage. Carry on walking along the road until it makes a sharp

turn to the left, continue straight ahead here through a gate onto a walled green lane. Follow the lane to its end and cross the stile, keeping to the wall on the right until it turns right, when you should continue straight ahead to another stile in the centre of the next wall. Cross the stile and head over the field opposite towards the far left corner where another stile takes you across the foot of the adjacent field before climbing yet another stile on the right. You are now on rather rough ground at the top of Plum Buttress which was seen earlier from below and it is advisable to keep strictly to the path. Follow the path to the left and upon reaching a small valley bear right, down the side before doubling back to cross a stile in a fence at the valley bottom. From here the path follows the valley down to rejoin the Monsal Trail at a stile by a bridge. Turn left here and retrace your steps along the trackbed until your way is barred at the end of the trail. Descend once more to the dale bottom via the steps on the left of the viaduct. All that now remains is the pleasant walk along the river bank back to the Wye Dale car park.

WALK 11

ILAM, THE MANIFOLD VALLEY, WETTON, ALSTONEFIELD, MILLDALE AND DOVEDALE

This is a lengthy walk, but worth the effort, taking in three interesting villages and arguably two of the most attractive dales. It starts at Ilam, a model village rebuilt in the 1820s in the fashionable Tudor Gothic style, and follows the course of the River Manifold for a short way before climbing high above the valley, only to descend again to the track of the former Manifold Valley Light Railway. From there it once again climbs out of the valley to visit the villages of Wetton and Alstonefield, crossing a series of fields inbetween after which it drops sharply to Milldale at the head of Dovedale. The remainder of the walk is relatively easy, passing through the dale as far as Thorpe Cloud and eventually back to Ilam.

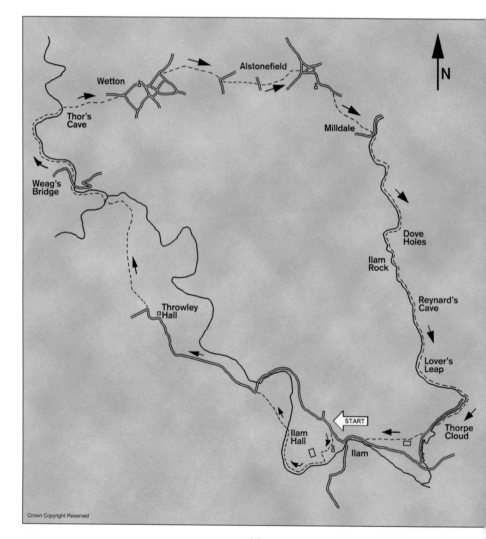

Map:
Ordnance Survey Outdoor Leisure Map 24.

Start:
Ilam village centre. Map ref. SK 135 509

Directions:
Ilam can be reached from the Ashbourne/Leek road via Blore or from the Ashbourne/Buxton road via Thorpe. Parking is available beside the road in the centre of the village.

Distance:
Approximately 12 miles (19km).

Duration:
Allow five-and-a-half to six hours inclusive of lunch for this walk and longer if intending to visit churches etc..

Refreshments:
Ye Olde Royal Oak at Wetton or *The George* at Alstonefield.

Ilam

The land surrounding Ilam was given to Burton Abbey in 1004 AD by a Saxon theyn or warrior named Wulfric Spott as penance for his part in the massacre of a number of Danes during 1002 AD. After the dissolution of the monastries, in 1546 the Ilam estate was given to John Port who built the first hall and whose family lived there until 1809. The name Ilam is derived from a Saxon word meaning 'at the hills' and the village is interesting, not least for its architectural style. It is perhaps somewhat out of place here within the Peak District, having been rebuilt in the Alpine style between 1821 and 1826 by Mr Jesse Watts Russell, a wealthy businessman. Head for the gates of Ilam Hall and take the road to the left of them. Almost immediately take a gated lane on the left which is sign-posted 'the Church and Hall'. When the church is reached bear right and facing you is what is left of Ilam Hall. It was rebuilt by Mr Watts Russell in spectacular Tudor Gothic style incorporating towers and turrets at the same time as the village. Now a Youth Hostel it is only a quarter of its original size having been partly demolished in 1934.

The church is very much older than the present hall and incorporates both Saxon and Norman features. It was restored in 1618 jointly by the Squires of Throwley, Ilam and Castern; Richard Meverell, Robert Port and Nicholas Hurt respectively. Their initials can be seen above the chapel door in the south wall of the church. Subsequently, in 1884 it was extensively renovated and the octagonal mausoleum was added. Parts of the walls are Saxon, as is the blocked doorway to the right of the main door and there are two Celtic crosses in the churchyard. The font is Norman and is engraved with scenes from the life of St. Bertram or Bertelin. In the Chapel of St. Bertram is the 9th century cover of his tomb and his shrine which was built about 1386.

St. Bertram

Alleged to have been the son of a Mercian King, Bertram is said to have travelled to Ireland around 700 AD in order to get married. He was returning with his wife when she gave birth to a son in a nearby forest. Bertram left them to go for food but when he returned he discovered that both wife and child had been eaten by wolves. Stricken with grief, Bertram renounced his inheritance and became a hermit, devoting the rest of his life to prayer and meditation. He lived locally and converted many people from the area to Christianity. In medieval times he became very popular and many miracle cures were claimed by pilgrims who crawled through the holes in the sides of his shrine. Even today people are still making pilgrimages to his tomb in the hope of receiving his favours.

Also in the chapel and dated 1626, is the alabaster memorial of Robert Meverell and his wife who lived at nearby Throwley Hall. Hanging above the entrance to the Chapel is a rare relic of an ancient peakland custom. In the past, if a girl died whilst being betrothed to be married, paper wreaths were made to be carried at her funeral and afterwards they were hung in the church. They were known as Virgin Crants or 'maidens garlands' and only one other example now remains, this can be found in the church of the Holy Trinity at Ashford-in-the-Water.

Paradise Walk

From the church go down to the river bank. Opposite there is an old packhorse bridge which is known as St. Bertram's Bridge and is thought to have been the main entrance into the original village. Turn right here and follow the riverside path which, typical of Victorian romanticism, was named 'Paradise Walk'. On the right there is a shallow cave complete with a carved rock desk and seat. It is alleged that 250 years ago, the author William Congreve wrote his comedy 'The Old Bachelor' here whilst staying at the old hall. Consequently it has become known as 'Congreve's Study' or 'Congreve's Grotto'. Doctor Samuel Johnson was also a visitor here and is believed to have derived inspiration from the valley for part of his novel 'Rasselas' which was published in 1759. He apparently wrote it during the evenings of just one week after his mother died, in order to settle her debts and pay for her funeral expenses.

Adjacent to the cave the Rivers Manifold and Hamps emerge from 'boil holes' after travelling for almost five miles underground. Only in exceptionally wet weather do the rivers flow above ground. A little further on is the 'Battle Cross', named once again by the Victorians. It is a Celtic cross which was unearthed in the foundations of a cottage during the rebuilding of the village. It dates from about 1050 and is thought to relate to the skirmishes between the Danes and the Saxons.

Continue to follow the riverside path until, after crossing a stile, you reach the second bridge. Cross the river bed here and begin to climb diagonally right up the fields opposite. Pass just below Rushley Farm, turning left at the road and immediately right to climb gently up the side of the valley on a narrow metalled lane.

As you climb higher the views open up and one can see far into the distance. The impressive house across the valley is Castern Hall, part of which is believed to have been a religious property owned by Burton Abbey. Nicholas Hurt bought the estate in 1560 and the family still reside there today. Eventually the lane brings you to Throwley Hall which was built in 1603. The land here was acquired by the Meverell family as early as 1203 and the last occupant of the hall was Robert Meverell who died in 1626. His body lies together with that of his wife in the church at Ilam. Though derelict, the remains of the building are attractive and are now protected by English Heritage.

Follow the lane to Throwley Hall Farm where the farmer is concentrating on beef production and has a fine herd of Charolais cattle. As you approach the farm the barn facing you is all that remains of two cottages which formed part of the old hamlet of Throwley and may now house some magnificent Charolais bulls. Having passed through two gates between the farm buildings, enter the farmyard on the right and pass through a stile immediately on the left. Take the footpath beyond this stile and walk up the field, heading diagonally right towards the corner of a wall. Before reaching the wall you will come upon a farm track which should be followed up the field, round the corner of the wall and eventually to a stile in another wall ahead. Having crossed the wall, the world opens up to you once more as the path continues straight ahead and breasts the top of the hill. Walk alongside the wall on the left, downhill until you reach a sign-post then turn right and follow the valley bottom which eventually becomes a dirt track. Look to your right here, where evidence can be clearly seen all the way down the hill of the medieval 'ridge and furrow' strip field system. Nearer the bottom, where the hill is steeper, terraces or 'lynchets' were constructed in order to maximise use of the land.

Continue along the track towards the massive limestone cliff of Beeston Tor where, hidden amongst the trees is St. Bertram's Cave, once used by Stone Age hunters as they followed the herds of deer and bison. It was here during excavation of the cave in 1924 that a most important discovery was made. A horde of forty-nine, ninth century Anglo-Saxon silver coins was found together with three gold rings and two silver brooches. These are now held in the British Museum.

The Manifold Valley Light Railway

In the valley bottom, at the confluence of the Hamps and Manifold, you join the trackbed of the old Manifold Valley Light Railway. Opened in 1904, it was the first to be built under the Light Railways Act of 1896, but it was never a commercial success. It had a 2'6" gauge track and had to use a special adapter trolley in order to carry conventional wagons on the line. The railway ran for eight miles between the village of Waterhouses in the Hamps Valley and Hulme End at the northernmost point of the Manifold Valley. It was originally intended to extend the line further north via Longnor and on to Buxton, but its failure to make money cut short the plans and the railway closed down in 1934. Subsequently the line was bought for £6000 by Staffordshire County Council, who then resurfaced the track and created what was to be the first bridleway along the route of a disused railway trackbed, calling it 'The Manifold Way'.

At the junction of the Hamps and Manifold Valleys was Beeston Tor Station. There was little in the way of comfort provided at the stations at that time and here an enterprising farmer set up a refreshment room for the benefit of visitors. It still stands on the left of the track to this day, although very much dilapidated.

The route is now via the Manifold Way and the first junction is at Weag's Bridge where Grindon Station was located. Grindon village, like most of its neighbours is high up on the plateau and is some considerable distance away. The remoteness of the line from the main areas of population was undoubtedly the reason for the railways lack of success.

Weag's Bridge used to carry the old packhorse route from Grindon to Alstonefield but it is now a road which can be quite busy at weekends so take care when crossing. Still following the Manifold Way, the valley now becomes more dramatic as it closes in between 300 foot cliffs and soon the site of another station is reached at Ladyside, where a sign-post indicates 'Thor's Cave' over a footbridge to the right. The station was intended to serve the village of Wetton but tended to be used rather more by visitors to the cavern.

Thor's Cave

Thor's Cave makes quite a dramatic sight with its huge gaping mouth high up on the limestone crag. In fact it is not very deep now, being very much the remnant of a large cave system which has gradually been eroded away over the years. Judging by the relics that were found here during the last century however, it would seem that it has been regarded as quite a desirable residence over a considerable period of ancient history.

The Wetton village schoolmaster, Samuel Carrington, a keen amateur archaeologist, spent much of his time investigating various sites in the locality and here he discovered a wide range of artefacts dating from about 5000 BC through to Roman times. They included flint arrow heads, iron adzes, bone combs, bronze jewellery, iron tools, pottery and coins.

In the 1920s a local eccentric founded a druidic cult which attracted members from all over the country. They held an annual ceremony called Gorseddau at which they would process from Wetton to the cave and on these occasions thousands of people would flock to the area just to watch them.

Make your way over the bridge and up through the trees in the direction of Wetton. Several footpaths go to Thor's Cave from here and the view is rewarding but be careful, the rocks are extremely slippery, especially in wet weather. When you emerge from the trees continue onwards across the fields until you reach a stile in a wall on the outskirts of Wetton village. Turn right after crossing the stile and take the road straight ahead through the village.

Wetton

Wetton today has taken advantage of its central location to promote the tourist industry and it has become very popular with holidaymakers and day trippers alike. The abundance of camping and caravan sites has not, as yet, spoilt the village itself which is quiet and has a clean appearance. The majority of the houses and farms date from the eighteenth century although a few, Manor House Farm and Hallow Grange for example, were built in the 1600s. This location seems to have been important to mankind from very early times however. The schoolmaster Samuel Carrington, mentioned earlier, discovered the foundations of many houses at nearby Borough Fields, a site that is now thought to be the remains of an abandoned Romano/British settlement.

He also found and excavated a number of small burial mounds in the area. A short distance away to the south of the village is Long Low, one of the oldest and most interesting examples of a prehistoric barrow in England. Dating from about 1600 BC, it comprises two burial mounds connected by a long bank. In one of the mounds a burial chamber was found containing thirteen human skeletons together with animal bones and flint tools.

Near the end of the road go right and walk through the churchyard of St. Margaret's. The church was rebuilt in 1820 on the site of a much earlier construction; the tower is thought to be 14th century. In the churchyard, the tomb decorated with seashells and fossils is that of the schoolmaster, Samuel Carrington. Pass straight through the churchyard and turn right at the road. On your right now is Ye Olde Royal Oak where lunch can be obtained if desired.

From the inn take the road opposite and walk down this until at the second junction on the right, you pass through a stile and proceed diagonally across the field to the opposite corner. Make your way via a series of wall stiles over the fields before entering a green lane where a right turn eventually leads to Brook Lodge at a bend in a narrow road at the valley bottom.

Turn right at the road but almost immediately leave it by way of a stile on the left, to join a footpath which traverses the fields with regular sign-posts indicating 'Alstonefield' to guide the way. Cross the road once more and climb straight up the hill, eventually crossing the village sports field and entering Alstonefield by the school. Cross the road carefully and walk down the narrow road opposite, keeping right at the junction to pass the tea room before arriving at the village green.

Alstonefield

Alstonefield has been a settlement since very early times. It was first recorded in 892 AD, but in the Domesday Book it was referred to as Aenestanefelt which roughly translated meant 'land free from woodland'. It is an attractive village made up mostly of buildings about 250 years old, although the Hall is dated 1587. The village green tends to get a little crowded with walkers and cyclists when the weather is favourable, due mainly to the refreshments available from The George an 18th century coaching inn.

Leaving the village green, take the Milldale road to the right, which takes you past the Hall and eventually to St Peter's Church which is well worth a visit. It has a variety of architectural styles dating from as early as 1300, and the chancel was rebuilt in 1590. There are a number of fragments of Saxon crosses, both in the churchyard and incorporated into the walls. Inside the church there is a bowl from a Saxon font and some striking 16th century wood carving. Also of interest is the Cotton family pew, a box pew commissioned by Charles Cotton senior who lived at Beresford Hall which stood not far away near Beresford Dale.

Milldale

Continue on past the church and where a track joins the road from the right, pass through a stile and take the footpath down the field and over a stile at the bottom left. Head diagonally cross the next field and pass through another stile before commencing the steep descent into the hamlet of Milldale. Milldale lies in a charming setting at the northern end of Dovedale and is relatively unspoilt due in the main to its inaccessibility for coaches. Such is the reputation of the dale that, if it were possible to manoeuvre a coach around the narrow roads, someone would certainly attempt to do so. Even so, its location ensures a steady stream of trippers whenever the weather is favourable. The farms and cottages are mostly of sixteenth and seventeenth century origin and as the name suggests there was once a mill here, but little remains of it now. The mill stable has been converted into an information barn which tells the story of the hamlet, its past and present and also of some of the characters who have lived there. It is quite interesting and is worth spending a few minutes over before setting off into the dale.

For most of its length, the River Dove forms the county boundary and as you cross to the east bank you are leaving Staffordshire and entering Derbyshire. The bridge itself is an old packhorse bridge which has become known as Viator's Bridge after the character Viator, friend of both Izaak Walton and Charles Cotton who in their famous book *The Compleat Angler*, is alleged to have said of the bridge, 'Why a mouse can hardly go over it, it is but two fingers broad'. The reason for Viator's exclamation is obvious, packhorse bridges were built only sufficiently wide enough to allow the passage of the mules and with low parapets, above which the panniers could be safely transported.

Dovedale

Dovedale is undoubtedly one of the finest beauty spots in the Peak and is justly renowned for its scenic views. The tree-lined river now gently flows beneath towering limestone cliffs and pinnacles but it must have been a torrent of tremendous force when, at the end of the last Ice Age, it formed these fantastic shapes by erosion of soft materials leaving the columns of harder rock which we see today.

Lord Byron wrote, 'Was you ever in Dovedale? I assure you there are things in Derbyshire as noble as in Greece or Switzerland.' Byron was not alone in singing the praises of the area and subsequently the Victorians came flocking here in great numbers and in typical fashion set about romanticising the dale by giving exaggerated or biblical names to many of the rock features. This served only to enhance further its attractiveness in the minds of the public and its popularity has remained to this day. There are of course two sides to every coin and the constant stream of visitors is considered by many to intrude upon the natural peace and tranquillity usually associated with the southern peak.

Having crossed the bridge, turn right and follow the wide and well-used footpath through the dale with Ravens Tor rising steeply beyond the river on the right. Soon the gaping mouths of the Dove Holes appear ahead of you and as you pass Nabs Dale on the left they can be seen at close quarters. Now only two shallow depressions in the rock face, they are the remnants of what must have been a massive cave system gouged from the limestone by the swirling glacial meltwaters.

Continuing on past the caves, shortly you will come to a footbridge over the river. The bridge is the start of a path which leads to Hall Dale on the right and should be ignored. Just beyond the bridge, you cannot fail to see Ilam Rock, a huge limestone column standing impressively on the opposite side of the river whilst on the left is Pickering Tor.

A little further on you come to Lion's Head Rock where the rock wall on the left bulges out towards the trail. Look carefully as you approach for it is said to resemble the head of a lion when viewed from a certain angle. Before long you enter 'The Straits', where the dale narrows and the sides are so steep that the path takes to a boardwalk placed along the edge of the river to help keep one's feet dry. Even so, when it is in spate, the river can easily rise above it making passage difficult. Having negotiated The Straits, pick up the footpath once more and after about 200 yards look out for an erosion control notice attached to a fence on the left.

Reynard's Cave

The fence and notice are placed here to deter people from climbing the scree up to Reynard's Cave, yet another unusual rock formation that attracts many visitors. No longer quite as big as it was originally, Reynard's Cave is really only the remnant of an enormous cave system which has collapsed leaving a small rock shelter in front of which is a superb natural rock arch. People have been coming here for years to scramble up the dale side to see the view through the arch. If you choose to do so take care, the loose rock can be very unstable and should you slip a serious injury could result. There used to be a lady who sold postcards and refreshments here. Her name was Annie Bennington and for 60 years she walked from Milldale each day carrying her wares plus a long rope which she fastened at the mouth of the cave and charged people a penny a time to use it to assist in their ascent.

It is said that in 1761 a gentleman intent upon impressing his lady attempted to take them both up the slope on his horse. Due to the steepness of the climb as they neared the top the horse overbalanced backwards and the pair were thrown. The horse was quite unhurt and made its way down without any difficulty but its master received head injuries which rendered him unconscious and from which he died two days later. As for the lady, she was remarkably fortunate, escaping with only minor cuts and bruises when her long hair caught in a thorn bush and saved her from tumbling all the way to the floor of the dale.

Moving on, you next come to Sharplow Dale on the left followed by the Tissington Spires, more limestone pinnacles, also on the left. On the right the large buttress standing alone is Jacob's Ladder. The path now begins to rise sharply away from the river to pass over the headland known as Lover's Leap where, like so many others, a girl is supposed to have thrown herself to her death after being abandoned by her lover. As you descend from the headland more limestone towers can be seen amongst the trees on the Staffordshire bank, these are named the Twelve Apostles and the huge crag shortly afterwards is Dovedale Castle Rocks.

Thorpe Cloud

The dale begins to open out a little now and soon the river bends to the right at the entrance to Lin Dale on the left. Here are the famous stepping stones featured in so many pictures of Dovedale. Do not cross the river here, but continue along the less well-used path on the Derbyshire bank. This is better than walking on the tarmacced lane and the stepping stones may be submerged if the river is high anyway. Thorpe Cloud is now on your left, a 942 foot conical hill guarding the southern entrance to Dovedale. The name 'Thorpe' has its origins in a Danish settlement which was hereabouts long ago and 'Cloud' is derived from the old English 'clud' which meant hill. The view from the top is superb, however, if you should decide upon the climb, be careful as the path has become much eroded with the wear and tear of visitors' feet. When a bridge is reached at the foot of the Cloud, cross to the lane and turn left.

A large car park has been established on the left, it is somewhat unsightly but does provide a public toilet which may be a welcome sight at this stage of the day. Take the footpath that leaves the lane opposite the toilets and pass through some trees into fields by the Izaak Walton Hotel, much changed from the day when Walton actually stayed there.

Pass behind the hotel, crossing two stiles and make your way in more or less a straight line over the fields with the sharp outline of Bunster Hill to the right. As the path converges with the road on the left look out for a stile and take care as you pass through the hedge into traffic. Cross the road and walk to your right making for the somewhat elaborate Gothic Cross which was erected by Jesse Watts Russell in 1840 in memory of his wife and marks the centre of Ilam village. From here make your way back to your car and home.

WALK 12

WIN HILL CIRCULAR

This walk, rather than climbing to the summit of Win Hill, makes a circuit of both the high and low ground surrounding it. The location of Win Hill is such that you do not have to gain a great deal of height in order to take advantage of the superb views in all directions. The walk sets out from Hope, an interesting village not far from the Roman Fort at Brough and the early stages retrace the route of one of their roads up the side of the Vale of Edale. It then descends into Woodlands Valley and follows the banks of the Ladybower Reservoir before climbing once more over to the Hope Valley and returning via the hamlet of Aston to Hope itself.

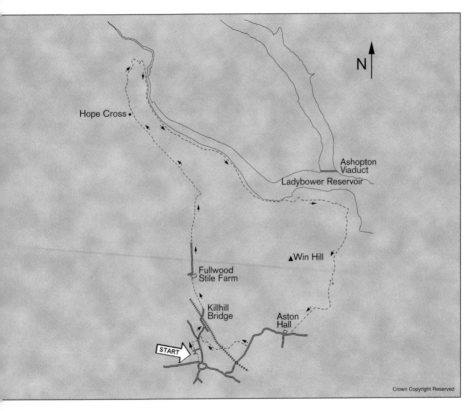

Crown Copyright Reserved

Map:
Ordnance Survey Outdoor Leisure Map 1

Start:
Hope car park.
Map reference SK 172 835

Directions:
Hope is located on the A625 approximately 6 miles east of Chapel-en-le-Frith. The car park is situated on the south side of the road close to the church.

Distance:
Approximately 9 miles (14.5km).

Duration:
Approximately four-and-a-half hours.

Refreshments:
A packed lunch will be required on this walk.

Hope Village

The village of Hope was originally Saxon, having been founded in the ninth or tenth century. By the time William the Conqueror invaded in the eleventh century it was already one of the largest parishes in England and many of its buildings reflect its long history. The Post Office and the *Cheshire Cheese* pub on the Edale road are both of sixteenth century origin whilst the church is, by and large, fourteenth century. Hope was one of the earliest centres of Christianity in the Dark Peak, a church and priest being recorded here in the Domesday Book. However it is certain that worship in some form or other took place on this site many years before. There are some of the finest Celtic gargoyles to be seen incorporated in the outer walls indicating perhaps that by mixing the old pagan symbols with those of the new Christian religion, the builders were hedging their bets a little. On the south side of the church stands a large red gritstone Saxon cross which was re-erected here in 1850 after it was found in two pieces being used as a door lintel in the original village school, having been there since the mid-1600s. Nearby is the stump of the Eccles Cross, thought to have been a medieval wayside cross and there is a Norman font inside the church. In a field close to the church an early Norman motte and bailey castle once stood.

The word 'Hope' was originally used to describe a side valley, in this case it probably referred to the Vale of Edale which starts here. The name was obviously adopted for the village which grew up at the entrance to the vale and with the passage of time, has now been accepted as the name of the main valley too.

Take the Edale Road opposite the church and walk past the school playing fields on the left before turning off at the road to Killhill Bridge on the right. After a short distance, pass under the railway bridge and turn left. Continue walking along the road until you reach the gates of 'Homestead' where you bear left again down the drive, towards a pair of cottages. Pass through the stile at the side of the right hand cottage to enter a field. Go straight ahead across the field keeping to the wall on your right.

Bloody Battle

There are now good open views on the left towards Lose Hill, pronounced 'loose'. At 1563 feet, Lose Hill together with the 1523 foot Win Hill dominate the surrounding area. Legend has it that the names are derived from a battle that took place here in 626 AD between King Edwin of Northumbria and King Cuicholm of Wessex. It seems that the battle took place following an unsuccessful assassination attempt on Edwin in which his friend and right-hand man was killed. The opposing armies were camped on each of the hills and when the fighting was finally over Edwin was victorious. Henceforth Edwin's hill was known as 'Win' and Cuicholm's as 'Lose'. This story may have been given credence by the close proximity of the 'Grey Ditch', an earthwork consisting of a rampart and ditch which is located above nearby Bradwell. It is believed to have been constructed about a hundred years later as the boundary between Northumbria and Mercia, the kingdom of Offa of Offa's Dyke fame, who had by then established himself as the most powerful king in England.

The truth, unfortunately, appears to be rather more mundane. The word Win is derived from 'Withie', a willow sapling, therefore Win Hill must have been a source of Willow trees at one time. Lose Hill's origin is perhaps even more down to earth. Lose, meant 'pigsty' so there is a fair probability that a pigsty was located on or near the hill sometime in the past. Oh well! So much for romance.

Doctor's Gate

Having traversed the field as far as Fullwood Stile Farm, climb the stile in the wall on the right and bear left through the farmyard onto a track which rises gradually to the right. You are now walking upon the route of the old Roman road which connected the forts of avio at Brough in the Hope Valley and that of Melandra or Ardotalia as it is more correctly known, near Glossop. Contrary to popular belief the Romans did not always build their roads in dead straight lines, particularly when confronted with the sort of difficult terrain which they encountered in the Peak District. Known as 'Doctor's Gate' after a Doctor who was Vicar of Glossop towards the end of the fifteenth century, the road travelled south from Glossop along the route of the Snake Pass Road before climbing up to Hope Cross, a drovers guide-post, and then descending via Aston into the Hope Valley. There have been many reports of ghostly Roman soldiers being seen along the route of this road but none quite so dramatic as that experienced by four climbers one night in 1932. Apparently, whilst resting in the vicinity of Hope Cross they were amazed (if not alarmed) to see an entire Legion of Centurions marching past them. Less spectacular but perhaps no less eerie, many people claim to have heard strange regular clanking noises whilst walking along this route for which they could find no logical explanation. It has been suggested that this is the sound made long ago by Legionnaires armour as they marched between the two forts.

When you come to a gate a choice of route can be made, either to stay on the track and follow the line of the Roman road as it climbs gradually up the hillside, or to leave the track by the footpath on the right which is a much stiffer climb but has the advantage of bringing you to the ridge much sooner and is therefore far more rewarding in terms of the views which it commands.

Peveril Castle

As you ascend the hillside a wonderful panorama opens up to you. Turning and looking back, the village of Bradwell can be seen across the valley beyond Hope. Looking west, down the Hope Valley is Castleton above which stands the keep of Peveril Castle. The castle was built in 1076 by William Peverel, the legitimate son of William the Conqueror as his administrative base when he served as bailiff of the royal forest of the peak. It is mentioned in the Domesday Book making it one of the oldest stone-built castles in England although there was probably an earlier castle there even before the Conquest. In 1175 the castle was repossessed by King Henry II and was used as a royal hunting lodge. He subsequently became a regular visitor on hunting trips, as were Kings Henry III and Edward III.

Ancient Hill Fort

On the right of Lose Hill one can see the length of the Vale of Edale with Edale itself and Upper Booth in the distance. The highest point along the ridge which extends from Lose Hill is the well-known 'shivering mountain', Mam Tor, topped with an ancient hill fort. It has a double ditch and bank defensive rampart and is thought to have been occupied during both the Bronze and Iron Ages. Fragments of pottery and other relics dating from between 1000 and 650 BC were found during excavations there. On the other side of the Vale of Edale, above Edale Village is the Kinder Plateau with Kinder Scout, at 2088 feet the highest point in the whole of the Peak District.

If you have elected to leave the track and climb the hillside via the footpath, as you near the top you will meet a broad, well-used path running from right to left in front of a plantation. To the right is the summit of Win Hill but rather than subject yourself to another climb turn left and take it easy on the straight and level footpath. After the exertions of the climb it is a pleasant walk beside the plantation still enjoying the views to the left.

Hope Cross

Eventually the Roman road which you left earlier joins the footpath from the left and you are faced with an unusual guide-post. It is a rough hewn stone pillar standing about seven feet high with a flat, square stone on the top. Known as 'Hope Cross', it was erected originally in 1737 and marked the crossing of two important packhorse routes. Each side of the capping stone is engraved with the name of a local town to direct the drovers of the time. Unfortunately the craftsman who created it was either semi-literate or simply made a mistake, spelling Sheffield with only one 'f'. To make matters worse, during the Second World War it was taken down and buried so as not to be of any help to the enemy in the event of an invasion and later, when it was re-erected, the capping stone was replaced ninety degrees out of position so that the place names face the actual direction of the destination. When it was first erected it would have been used by going to the right of the place name to which you were headed. Another reminder of the days when horsepower meant exactly that, is the gully to the left which is called Jaggers Clough after the drovers who used to lead the packhorse trains, and were commonly known as 'Jaggermen'. The name was derived from the German 'Jaeger' ponies which they often used.

From here the way forward is through the gate and along the track to the stile that can be seen by the sign-post on the skyline where you turn right in the direction of Hagglee Ford, back to the edge of the plantation. You can however take a small short cut by following the somewhat uneven path which runs beside the plantation. When the two paths meet go through the gate into the plantation itself where the track is rather rough and can be very slippery when wet. It descends steadily through the trees, gradually turning to the right until it becomes a more well-defined forest road as it nears the bottom of Woodlands Valley.

Ladybower Reservoir

When the road makes a sharp left hand turn, carry straight on over a stile by a gate onto a wide earth road which runs along the side of the valley. This is another forest road which is used only by the forestry workers, therefore traffic is infrequent and one can walk along it at leisure. Before long the River Ashop below begins to widen out until it fills the whole of the valley bottom and becomes the Ladybower Reservoir. The reservoir stretches for approximately two miles along the Woodlands Valley and a further three miles along the Derwent Valley. It was the last in a series of three reservoirs that were built in the vicinity to supply the needs of Sheffield, Derby and Leicester. It was begun in 1935 and officially opened ten years later. Over that period 100,000 tons of clay and 1,000,000 tons of earth were removed. Sadly, it also necessitated the destruction of the small hamlet of Ashopton together with thirteen farms. The reservoir covers an area of 504 acres, holds 6,300 million gallons of water and has a maximum depth of 135 feet.

The walk by the reservoir can be very pleasant on a warm summer's day, quiet and unhurried and somehow far from the everyday bustle typified by the rushing of the traffic on the A57 over the valley. It is fairly level for much of the way but of course we do eventually have to climb back out of the valley again. Follow the road until, in sight of Ashopton Viaduct, at the end of a wall on your left, you turn right on a path beside an area used by forestry workers for the storage of their equipment and timber. After a few yards turn left on a green track which climbs gradually through mature trees until at a junction of forest roads, you bear right and almost immediately, at a second junction bear right again. High over to the left is Derwent Edge crowned with a number of unusual rock formations, the Cakes o' Bread the Salt Cellar, Wheel Stones and those nearest to you are the Hurkling Stones.

Dambusters

The trees are quite young here and consequently the visibility is good. Looking down to the left one can get a good view of most of the reservoir, its dam and Yorkshire Bridge, which was originally built in 1695 and was so named because it led to that county. On the far side of Ashopton Viaduct is Derwent Dale where the remainder of the reservoir is situated, together with the other two in the series, first Derwent and then Howden. The Derwent Reservoir is of course well known for being used by the Lancaster bomber crews to practice the dropping of the bouncing bomb of 'Dambusters' fame during the Second World War.

Continue the gradual ascent along the road until it levels out and after passing through stand of mature trees cross another path descending the hill at Parkin Clough. In a few yards the forest ends and when you step from the trees the world opens out to you once more. As you contour the hill ahead a different view presents itself every few yards. Slightly ahead of you is Bamford Moor and Bamford Edge behind which, in the distance, is Stanage Edge. In the valley below is first, the village of Bamford and then beyond that is Hathersage.

Continue walking around the hill, initially keeping a wall on your right. The path tends to be a little indistinct here, however if you maintain straight and level progress, before long you will encounter an obvious broad footpath descending from the right. Turn right, up this path until, when it reaches the wall you pass through a gap and turn left. Shortly the path becomes a broad well-defined track and once again the views are quite striking. Having moved round to the south of Win Hill the view has become much clearer and you can now see the course of the River Derwent running between Eyam Moor and Big Moor. Nether Padley and Froggatt villages can also be seen with above them, the Edges of Froggatt, Curbar and Baslow stretching away into the distance.

The path eventually descends to a high wall where there is a stile. Climb over the wall by this stile and walk down the field beside a wooded ditch on the left. Go through a further two stiles, walking down the fields in more or less a straight line and soon you will emerge by the side of a cottage onto a narrow road at Aston.

Aston

Although only a tiny hamlet, Aston must have been a place of some significance in the past. As stated earlier, the Roman road passed through here on its way to and from Navio and in 926 AD it was sufficiently important to be granted a Royal Charter by Athelstan along with much larger towns such as Bakewell, Hope and Ashford.

Turn right along the road and take a look at the building immediately on your right. This is Aston Hall, a sixteenth century manor house. Built in 1578, it has five bays and incorporates some unusual architectural features not typical of the period such as the arched doorway and the steeply pitched gable.

Follow the road between high banks with the gnarled roots of the old trees which flank it exposed on either side. When you come to the road to Farfield Farm by a bungalow on the right, take this and shortly bear left onto a track which skirts the farm. The path runs alongside a small caravan site on the left immediately after which you leave the track by a stile in the fence on the left. Proceed down the field to another stile in the hedge on the right. The route is obvious now, passing under the railway via kissing gates and a bridge, and crossing more stiles before coming out on a lane at the old mill which is now a private house. Turn right past the mill noting the now static and much deteriorated timber water wheel on the left. Follow the lane between mature trees to the junction with the Killhill Bridge road on which you walked earlier in the day. Turn left, and upon reaching the next junction, cross the road and take the footpath opposite. Turn left at the top of the field and then follow the path down to a road by the school house. Cross to the road opposite and, passing between the houses on the left, go through a heavy metal kissing gate and walk down the footpath to a similar gate to emerge on the main road in the centre of Hope village with the car park opposite and to the right.

55

WALK 13

WETTON MILL, ECTON AND WARSLOW

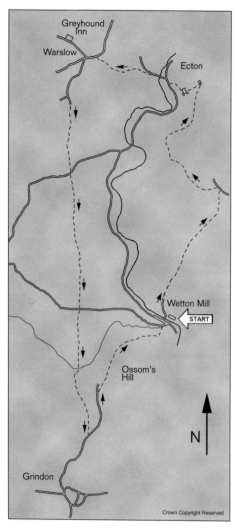

Crown Copyright Reserved

haunted *Greyhound Inn* before heading south over the fields adjacent to the Manifold, on an ancient footpath to Grindon. Before entering the village however, the route turns east to traverse Ossom's Hill and overlook the Wetton Mill Rock Shelter which, from Mesolithic to Bronze Age times, was a temporary home for the early inhabitants of the Peak District. Finally the path descends once more to the valley bottom at Wetton Mill.

Map:
Ordnance Survey Outdoor Leisure Map 24.

Start:
Wetton Mill. Map reference SK 095 561

Directions:
Head for Butterton, off the B5053 between Onecote and Warslow. From there Wetton Mill and the Manifold valley are clearly sign posted. Free parking is available by the side of the Manifold Way and you can park at the Mill but this is expensive.

Distance:
Approximately 6 miles (9.5km).

Duration:
Approximately 4 hours.

Refreshments:
The *Greyhound Inn* at Warslow.

Wetton Mill

Cross the river by the bridge towards the mill. Nowadays it is a tea room and frequently very busy but once it was a water-driven corn mill thought to date from the late sixteenth century. It certainly existed as early as 1617 but by the mid-1800s it had closed and there is now little evidence remaining of the original.

Turn left, away from the mill, after crossing the bridge and head for Dale Farm. Pass through the farmyard and walk up the valley towards a large outcrop of reef limestone known as 'the Sugar Loaf'. Bear left here and follow the path

This walk embraces the hills and countryside surrounding the upper Manifold Valley. The early stage takes in some outstanding views from Ecton Hill and then descends into the small hamlet of Ecton where the peace and tranquillity belies its industrial past. The story of the copper mines is quite remarkable and some unique records were set by the miners in their heyday. From there you climb out of the valley to visit the village of Warslow and the up the hill to a stile. Ignore the path which goes off to the left and walk alongside the wall on the right, still heading up the valley. At the end of the field pass through a gap in the wall and continue to follow it on the other side until you reach a stile by the side of a pond. Climb the stile onto a track and turn left towards Broad Ecton Farm but leave the track almost immediately by another stile on the left which gives access to a footpath to Summerhill Farm. Walk up the field with the wall on your right until you reach a stile which you should cross, then walk diagonally left, up the field to the opposite corner. Carry on in a straight line until you intersect a long wall which runs from top to bottom of the hill. Make a left turn here and follow the wall to the brow of the hill, pass through a convenient gap and start to walk slightly downhill to a further stile in a wall at the edge of the dale.

The Manifold Valley

The view from here is superb, on a clear day you can see for miles across the valley to the villages of Grindon, Butterton and Warslow and even further away, Morridge. Below you is Swainsley Hall sitting in a curve of the river where the Warslow Brook enters the valley. Just to the left is Swainsley Tunnel a reminder of the Manifold Valley Light Railway which ran beside the river.

Opened in 1904, the railway ran for eight miles between the village of Waterhouses in the Hamps valley and Hulme End at the northern end of the Manifold valley. It was never really a commercial success, the copper mines at Ecton that would have generated more than enough business, having closed long before it was built. The reason for the line's lack of success was that it was some considerable distance from the customers it intended to serve, that is the population of villages such as Butterton, Grindon, and Wetton, all situated on the plateau above the valley and not at all convenient.

There was a cheese factory at Ecton that used the line to send its products on the initial stage of the journey from here to London each day but this freight alone was hardly sufficient to sustain the business. There was some income from tourism but this was negligible and in 1934 it inevitably closed. It was subsequently bought by the Staffordshire County Council for the princely sum of £6000 and, showing considerable foresight, they resurfaced the trackbed for recreational purposes, creating the Manifold Way for the benefit of cyclists and walkers, the first linear park in the country.

The route now turns north beside the wall until, at the shoulder of the hill, the views become more extensive. Over to your right you can now see Hartington and straight ahead is Sheen with Longnor in the distance whilst to your left is Warslow which is much clearer from here, and is conspicuous by the very much out-of-place modern school.

Ecton

Below you is the wide sweep of Ecton Hill this part of which during the thirteenth century was a deer park. Though much recovered, it now bears the scars of many years of mining activity. Like most of the southern Peak, there was a certain amount of lead mining in Ecton, but here it was copper that brought fame and fortune to the village and was responsible for so many noteworthy events. In 1670, it was here that gunpowder was used for blasting for the first time in a British mine and in the eighteenth century the largest and deepest mine in Britain was here. There was an underground canal used for haulage and a thirty-two foot diameter water wheel which operated below ground to drain the lower levels. Eventually, this was replaced in 1788 by one of the first Boulton and Watt steam engines.

Copper had been extracted here in a small way as early as the beginning of the seventeenth century but this had long since ceased when, it is said, a Cornish miner who happened to be passing, found some copper ore lying on the ground and obtained a twenty-five year lease from the landowner, the Duke of Devonshire. Profits were low at first but eventually he discovered rich 'pipes' of copper so when the lease expired the Duke decided to take advantage of the finds and began to really exploit the reserves of ore.

Make your way carefully down the hillside to your left until you intersect another path which traverses the side of the hill. Turn right and when it forks, after turning the corner of the hill, take the upper path which picks its way around many old mineworkings towards a group of trees surrounding what appears to be an area of scree on the slope opposite. The hillside is covered with numerous old shafts which can be dangerous so please do not stray from the path. Eventually the path brings you to the site of a later mine, the remains of the buildings being clearly visible on the left. The ore from here was of a particularly high grade and reaped rich profits for the Duke. It is estimated that during the eighteenth century alone the royalties were worth some £1,350,000 and that from one year's profit the Duke was able to build The Crescent at Buxton. Much of the profit resulted from the Royal Navy's introduction towards the end of the seventeenth century, of sheathing the hulls of their ships with copper plate. Incidentally, it was as a result of this practice that the term 'copper bottomed' meaning safe or guaranteed was coined.

Deep Ecton

From this point, carry on up the hill towards a stone-built barn on the skyline. The barn has been built on the site of the engine house for what was the deepest mine, Deep Ecton. In the eighteenth century, at some 1380 feet, this was the deepest mine in Britain. If you stand here and look down into the valley bottom you can't help but be impressed when you consider that the mine descended a further 1000 feet below the level of the river.

The mine employed a workforce of about 300 people, men, women and children all toiling in what we would consider to be the most appalling conditions. It seems however to have been considered quite acceptable at the time, there being little or no unrest here. The men worked by candlelight in the deepest recesses of the mine earning just one shilling (five new pence) for each six hour shift. The women were employed to break the ore into manageable pieces whilst the children were used on the lighter tasks such as sorting and preparing the ore for transportation.

From the barn take the path on the left of the wall which goes straight down the hill towards the large house with the green copper spire. The house is considered to be something of a folly because of its unusual design but personally I find it quite charming. It was built in 1933, by Arthur Ratcliffe the Member of Parliament for Leek, who was said to be an eccentric. He apparently spent most of his time here and precious little in the House of Commons but who can blame him if he preferred to spend his time here rather than in London.

Cross the stile at the bottom of the hill, turn right past the house and follow the track down to the road in the valley bottom. Turn right and then left over the road bridge and start the climb up the other side but look out for a path which climbs the bank almost immediately on the left. The path climbs steeply at first and if you look over to your right, on the hillside across the road, you will see yet another legacy of the industrial past of Ecton, the rather less profitable lead mines. Follow the path up the fields to a barn and there take the right hand path to Hobcroft Farm. Upon reaching the farm climb the stile to the main road, turn left and walk the short distance into Warslow.

Warslow

Warslow was formerly an estate village belonging to the Harpur-Crewe family of Calke Abbey. North east of the village is Warslow Hall which once served as a shooting lodge for the family. The village was recorded in the Domesday Book as Wereslei. It is unusual in that some of the surrounding land was enclosed as early as 1548 long before the Enclosures Act of 1839.

Headless Horseman

At the road junction, turn right and walk up the main street to the *Greyhound Inn* which is on the right. An inn has stood on this site attending to the needs of travellers for many years, for this was once a busy coaching route. It is an ideal place to stop for lunch providing you are not of a nervous disposition for supposedly it is haunted by the ghost of a young servant girl dressed in typical eighteenth century clothing. There is little likelihood that you will encounter her whilst on this walk though, for she has only ever been seen late at night sitting quietly by the fireside. There is however, every possibility that you will come across another of the village's ghosts when you leave the inn, especially if you have lingered too long in the bar, for it is said that a headless horseman rides up and down the main street from time to time.

Return to the main road and at the junction turn right and cross over to the lane on the left by the village stocks. Walk down to the end of the lane and at Villa Farm carry straight on where a footpath is sign-posted. You are now following the route of an ancient holloway, a path so well used in times gone by that it has formed a sunken ditch, parts of which can still be seen here and there on the left. It proceeds almost due south towards Grindon, descending first to the Warslow Brook before climbing out of the valley to the Butterton/Hulme End road.

Having crossed the road, take the track opposite and as you do so look to your left at the 1212 foot Ecton Hill where you can clearly see where you walked earlier. At the gate to Kirksteads Farm bear right on a footpath which immediately drops to another brook before rising gently over fields towards Wallacre Farm and eventually to the Butterton/Wetton Mill road.

Cross the road to the footpath directly opposite and start to descend into the deep valley of the Hoo Brook, a tributary of the Manifold. After crossing the footbridges take the left hand path to Grindon. Climb steadily up the fields and eventually the tall landmark of Grindon church spire will come into view ahead.

Grindon

Recorded in the Domesday Book as 'Grendone', the name Grindon originates from the Old English, *grene dun*, which means green hill. During the severe winter of 1947 a tragedy occurred nearby when a Halifax bomber bringing relief supplies to the snowbound villages, crashed on Grindon Moor killing all occupants, the crew plus a number of sightseers and a contingent of press photographers. In the church there is a simple commemorative tapestry.

When the footpath meets a fenced lane, cross the stile and double back on yourself along the lane towards Ossom's Hill Farm. As you walk along the lane, look to your right to the south of Ossom's Hill where a dramatic view of Thor's Cave can be seen in the Manifold Valley in the distance.

Upon reaching Ossom's Hill Farm, bear right on a footpath which crosses a number of fields before traversing the north side of Ossom's Hill overlooking Waterslacks on the left. As you emerge from an area of scrub and small hawthorn bushes the Manifold Valley once again comes into view.

Wetton Mill Rock Shelter

Below you is Wetton Mill and above it, on the north side of Nan Tor, is Wetton Mill Minor Rock Shelter. This is in fact a series of small, shallow caves in which many artefacts have been found which indicate that they were probably used from as early as 5000 BC in the middle Stone Age, through to the Bronze Age, about 500 BC. There are a number of such caves located here alongside the Manifold, including Thor's Cave which was seen earlier. Nearby is the Elderbush Cave, which was inhabited by both humans and animals. Bones of such creatures as lion, hippopotamus, bison and hyena were found here together with tools made of flint and reindeer antler. The caves were used as temporary shelters by early tribes who at that time were nomadic, hunter/gatherers. They simply followed herds of deer and bison which provided them with most of their needs and took shelter wherever they could. It is possible that the caves became semi-permanent dwellings later because on the hillside above Wetton Mill is Mill Pot, a vertical pothole in which more Bronze Age relics were discovered. The findings suggest that it was probably used as a burial place by those who lived in the shelter below. If you care to take a closer look at the shelter it can be approached by a footpath from behind the mill.

Descend the hillside carefully, the footpath is steep in places, down to the footbridge and walk the last few yards down the road and across the ford to return to the car park on the Manifold Way.

WALK 14

FROGGATT EDGE, CURBAR EDGE AND
THE DERWENT VALLEY

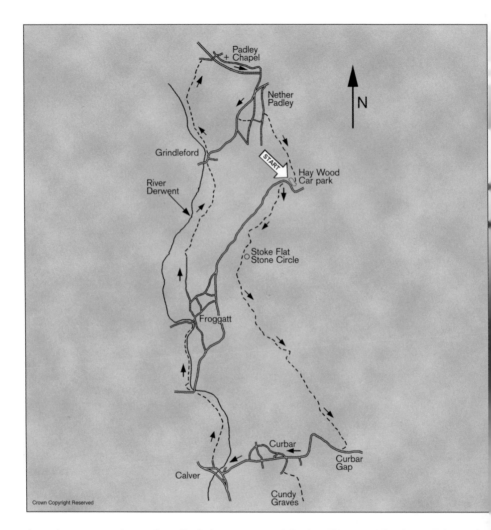

Crown Copyright Reserved

In stark contrast to the southern Peak there are no white limestone bluffs and buttresses to lighten the skyline in this area. The Derwent valley is skirted along the whole of its eastern side by dark brooding gritstone edges and for some twenty miles this rocky escarpment provides some of the finest climbing and linear walking in the area. Besides Froggatt and Curbar Edges it includes Derwent Edge, Stanage Edge and Millstone Edge to the north and Baslow Edge and Gardom's Edge to the south. This walk takes in not only the exhilaration of two high-level edges but also the very pleasant valley below, deeper and wider than those in the south. Here the River Derwent meanders lazily through picturesque fields and woodland.

Map:
Ordnance Survey Outdoor Leisure Map 24

Start:
Hay Wood car park and picnic site.
Map reference SK 256 776

Directions:
From Calver head north on the B6001 and turn right on the B6054. The car park is on the left a little over a mile beyond *The Chequers Inn*.

Distance:
Approximately 9 miles (14km).

Duration:
Five hours including lunch.

Refreshments:
The Bridge in Calver.

Setting out

Having parked your car, walk through the wood away from the entrance and leave at the opposite end via a deep gully to the road. Cross to a kissing gate a little to the right, and commence the gentle ascent up the lightly wooded slope onto Froggatt Edge. The sandy track upon which you are now walking was in medieval times a major thoroughfare which carried traffic of all kinds to Sheffield via Curbar Gap along both Froggatt and Curbar Edges.

Stoke Flat Stone Circle

Before long a kissing gate is reached and shortly after the gate look out for a standing stone amongst the bracken and ferns on the left. Take a closer look and you will see that this stone is part of a group forming a circle. This is Stoke Flat Stone Circle and is perhaps smaller than one might expect and therefore easily missed. It has stood here since the late Bronze Age, about 3000 years and was probably built by the Urn People, so called because of their practice of burying the ashes of their dead in upturned urns, many examples of which have been found on the moors hereabouts.

Flora's ghost

There are fine views of the Derwent Valley from most of the paths along the edges. From here you can look north towards Grindleford, Upper and Nether Padley and in the distance, Hathersage. Below you, across the valley, is the hamlet of Stoke nestling beneath the slopes of Sir William Hill. The large imposing building below is Stoke Hall, originally the home of Sir William Cavendish the grandson of Bess of Hardwick. He was a Royalist who fought in the battle of Marston Moor in 1644 and it is possible that it was he whom the hill was named after. The present building, now a hotel, was constructed in 1755 and almost from its completion has had a reputation for strange apparitions. Several guests have reported having seen a headless woman wearing an elaborate ball gown descending the staircase and rumours used to persist about a skull that haunted the servants' quarters on the upper floors. By far the most frequently told story though is that of Flora, a servant girl who was murdered, by a jealous lover. Her employers had thought so much of her that they erected a memorial statue of her in the garden when she died but they were somewhat alarmed when the hall was suddenly visited by a spate of bad luck and people claimed that the statue was seen to move after dark. The statue was moved to another part of the garden but its head was continually knocked off, probably by superstitious neighbours. Flora is still said to haunt the Hall to this day.

There is a choice of routes along Curbar Edge, either the broad sandy track over the moor or the more rewarding path that follows the very edge. From here you can see both Curbar and Calver in the valley and on a good day Stoney Middleton in Middleton Dale. On a warm, clear day this is a very pleasant walk but one can imagine the rigours of travel on such roads in the past. The open windswept moors, especially in wet or misty conditions are not the most attractive of places.

Millstones

As you walk along the edges, many discarded millstones can be seen below. At one time the production of millstones was a thriving and lucrative trade along all of the edges. To make transportation easier, they were carved and dressed on the spot, after which they would be assembled two at a time on an axle and rolled down the hill to a convenient position for loading on a cart. They were subsequently exported all over the world, even as far afield as Russia. Their principal use was for grinding corn and most of those that can be seen here are of the later, flat sided variety but there are a few about that have a curved face and these originate from a much earlier design. Towards the end of the eighteenth century cheaper stone became available from France and suddenly the bottom fell out of the industry, which accounts for their abandonment.

Curbar Gap

The southern end of Curbar Edge is marked by the road passing through the escarpment at Curbar Gap. Once again this is yet another ancient thoroughfare, this time from Middleton Dale across the Derwent at Calver and over the top to Sheffield and Chesterfield. This was an important trading route during the fifteenth century and has probably been in use since much earlier times. Having walked along the edges one can easily see why the road is located at this point, Curbar Gap providing a comparatively easy passage through the otherwise insurmountable gritstone outcrops. As if to illustrate this an old guide-post stands nearby, its lettering now worn and illegible, but it must have been a welcome sight to travellers making their way over the open moorland, indicating as it does the only way to the shelter of the valley.

Make your way down to the road and turn right in the direction of Curbar. Unfortunately there is no alternative but to use the road here and it does tend to get busy, particularly at weekends, so please take care and walk on the verges to avoid the traffic wherever possible. Close by the road you may see biblical texts carved into some of the larger boulders which are strewn around the hillside here. These were done by Edwin Gregory, a mole catcher and occasional Methodist preacher who, having recovered from a serious illness during the 1880s, spent much of his time carving the texts in thanksgiving for his deliverance.

The Cundy Graves

A little further down the hill however there are other, very different stones, a reminder of an earlier and much less happy occasion. Everyone knows of the 'Black Death', the great plague which swept the country claiming numerous lives during the years 1665/6 and indeed, the most famous tale of all, that of the bravery of the villagers of Eyam, only a short distance from here. What many may not be aware of is that the plague was not so uncommon in those days and that many small outbreaks used to occur intermittently; not really surprising when one considers the damp and insanitary conditions that many folk had to endure at the time.

Just such an outbreak occurred in the village of Curbar in 1632 when an entire family fell victim. Thomas Cundy, his wife Ada and their three children, Olive, Nellie and young Thomas who lived at nearby Grislow Farm were buried, as was the custom in those days, far away from the immediate area where people lived for fear of further infection. When you reach a sign-post on the left indicating a footpath to Baslow, take a small detour down the side road towards Lane Farm.

At the gate to Lane Farm, go over the stile on the left and across the field and on to the moor beyond. About fifty yards beyond, on the right lie the 'Cundy Graves'. All that remains as a memorial to the unfortunate Cundy family are five rough limestone slabs which were once crudely inscribed only with the initials of their occupants but now, even that all but obliterated by constant exposure to the elements. Were it not for the modern explanatory notice beside the footpath the graves would not be noticed and the Cundys forgotton for all time.

Retrace your steps now, but as you cross the field notice the curious square building with a stone slabbed conical roof in the garden of the house on the right. This was at one time the Curbar village lockup where offenders were kept whilst awaiting the assizes.

Upon returning to the road, continue down the hill and in Curbar itself, on the left of the road a circular pinfold can be seen. Pinfolds were to be found in most villages in the past. They were simply small, communal enclosures where anyone who came across any stray livestock could safely restrain the animals until such time that the owner could claim them.

Calver

When you reach Calver at the bottom of the hill *The Bridge* public house is facing you. This is an ideal place to stop for lunch if you care to do so. Cross the river bridge outside the inn on what was originally the main road through Calver. Due to its location at the junction of the turnpike and the trading route which passed over the edges, the village was quite busy with regular coaches passing through. There were two coach houses at that time, *The Bull's Head* and *The London Tavern* but both are now private houses called *Peak House* and *London House* respectively. The village was bypassed some years ago and consequently is now much quieter than it once was.

The name Calver was Calvoure in the Domesday Book which literally means 'calf slope', therefore one might assume that the rearing of cattle was a principal activity here at some time. Not quite so long ago cotton was the main industry as witnessed by the large mill by the riverside on the right.

Colditz

The present mill was built by Richard Arkwright in 1803 after the previous one, which dated from 1785, was burnt down in 1802. The Derwent, being the greatest of the peakland rivers, was what first attracted Arkwright to the idea of water power and prompted him to build his first mill beside the river at Cromford in 1771. Cotton production ceased here in 1923 but the building saw a brief moment of fame more recently when it was used as a look-alike for the German prison during the filming of the television series 'Colditz'. Interestingly, during the Second World War, lights were erected on the moors nearby in order to confuse the German bomber pilots into thinking they were over Sheffield and thereby diverting them away from the strategic sites in the city. Having crossed the bridge, continue along the road before turning right by the General Store, on the mill approach road. Keep straight on past the mill gates and follow the track towards a building with a bell tower on the roof. This was once a schoolhouse built by the mill owner for the benefit of his apprentices. Pass by on the right of the school and go through a kissing gate almost straight ahead to join a footpath which crosses a field towards a wider, tree-lined path beside the mill leat. From this section of the walk Curbar Edge can look quite magnificent in the afternoon sun. Carry on along the footpath and soon you will see the weir of the mill dam over to the right. If there has been recent rains and the water is high you will almost certainly hear it before you see it as the water cascades in white waves over the dam. As you pass the dam you will meet with the B6054 as it crosses the river at New Bridge. Cross the road and take the footpath immediately opposite which bears left at first but then turns right over a footbridge to run parallel with the River Derwent on its west bank.

River Derwent

The name Derwent is actually derived from Derventju which literally meant 'abounding in oaks' and was first recorded as Deorwentan in 1009. The river is deep and wide at this point with occasional trees overhanging the banks. The stillness of the water tends to attract ducks and other water fowl and the walk to Froggatt Bridge can be a very pleasant experience.

Froggatt

Froggatt Bridge is an elegant seventeenth century structure with a high pointed arch and a smaller one beside it. Upon arrival at the bridge leave the river bank by the step stile and cross to the other side into Froggatt. The place name was first recorded in 1225 as 'Froggecote', probably derived from Frogga Cot which meant Frog Cottage; possibly relating to its location beside the river.

Body Snatchers

Little more than a hamlet, Froggatt is nonetheless an attractive old place. Above the village, on the B6054, stands the two-hundred-year-old *Chequers Inn* which replaced an earlier fifteenth century one. The inn has a rather dubious claim to fame as it is reputed to have been a favourite resting place for body snatchers en route to Nether Padley where they apparently used to hide the corpses in the wood until they could be disposed of to unscrupulous doctors.

Turn left after crossing the bridge and walk down the road until you see Rose Cottage ahead of you. Go left by the cottage on a lane which soon becomes a footpath. Your way is now clear along what was once a turnpike road which ran the length of the valley. It passes through open fields at first, before entering ancient woodland which is now owned by the National Trust.

Once into the woods the path twists and bends and the odd muddy patch by a brook has to be negotiated, as well as the occasional fallen log but eventually you emerge at an open field. Cross the field beside the wall and pass through the stile and over the footbridge on the left. From this point, head across the field for the opposite corner, crossing the stile onto the B6001 road on the outskirts of Grindleford. As you do so, notice the old cottage across the road, this was once a toll house, a reminder that this was an important and well-used turnpike in the past.

If you wish, the walk can be shortened by approximately one-and-a-half miles from here by taking the rough road on the right which becomes a footpath climbing straight up through Hay Wood to the car park, otherwise....

Turn right towards Nether Padley, ignoring the rough road on the right and then carefully cross the road to pick up another footpath on the other side. This path once again follows the river until, having crossed a concrete bridge, you bear right up the field beside the wall, in the direction of Upper Padley. When you pass a wall joining from the right go diagonally right to a gap in the wall ahead of you. Passing through the wall, turn right and upon reaching the railway, cross the footbridge turning immediately right again to Padley Chapel which is on the left after 150 yards or so.

The Padley Martyrs

The Chapel was originally the gatehouse of Padley Hall which was built in 1415 by Robert Eyre when he married Joan Padley upon his return from Agincourt. The Hall has long since been demolished but the floor plan can be distinguished by the foundations alongside the chapel. The chapel too was thought to have been lost but it was rediscovered being used as a cow shed after the altar had been found by chance in 1933. Earlier it had been used as a store by the navvies building the Totley Tunnel.

Eventually the hall came into the ownership of the Fitzherberts, a staunch Catholic family. At a time when Mary Queen of Scots was imprisoned nearby, they were regarded with much suspicion and in 1571 Sir Thomas was arrested and sent to the Tower of London where, after thirty years of imprisonment, he subsequently died. In his absence his brother John looked after the hall and on February 2nd 1588, the manor was raided on the orders of the Lord Lieutenant of Derbyshire and two priests were found being sheltered by the family. They were promptly arrested on suspicion of celebrating Mass and were taken to Derby where, after a show trial, they were hung, drawn and quartered and their heads were displayed on poles in the city for all to see. Despite constant pressure from the crown, the family steadfastly refused to renounce Catholicism and eventually John was arrested and condemned to death but before the sentence could be carried out, he too died in prison. The chapel is now the object of a Roman Catholic pilgrimage each year in honour of 'The Padley Martyrs'.

Continue on past the chapel and the Railway Station beyond, turning right past the entrance to the 'Totley Tunnel'. The tunnel carries the railway line for over three miles beneath Totley Moor. Carry straight on up to the junction with the main road and turn right, crossing to the *Maynard Arms Hotel*. Shortly after the hotel turn left at a sign-post which indicates Froggatt Edge and Owler Bar. The path climbs steeply to an unmade road and continues almost opposite but a little to the left. This path also climbs steeply but not for too long and soon emerges at yet another unmade road. Turn left here and in about fifty yards, take the footpath on the right which rises gently through Hay Wood to return you eventually to the car park.